P9-CRQ-970

SHORT-TERM COUNSELING

CONTEMPORARY CHRISTIAN
COUNSELING

SHORT-TERM COUNSELING

DAVID DILLON, Ph.D.

CONTEMPORARY CHRISTIAN COUNSELING

— General Editor —
GARY R. COLLINS, PH.D.

Library of Congress Cataloging-in-Publication Data:

Dillon, David, 1941 Aug. 16–
    Short-term counseling / David Dillon.
        p.   cm. — (Contemporary Christian counseling)
    Includes bibliographical references and index.
    ISBN 0–8499–0775–6
    1. Pastoral counseling.   2. Short-term counseling—Religious aspects —Christianity.   I. Title.   II. Series; Contemporary Christian Counseling Series.
BV4012.2D56   1992
253.5—dc20   92–17491
                                                                    CIP

    59   LB   9 8 7 6 5 4 3

Printed in the United States of America

Contents

11.74

94141

Introduction

MY ROMANCE WITH SHORT-TERM COUNSELING began some years ago when a fellow counselor introduced to me the idea that helpers could direct a counselee in such a way that the counselee would improve whether the client complied with or defied the helper's directive. Surprised and somewhat skeptical, I started along a path of reading and attending seminars and workshops, as well as putting into practice short-term techniques. They worked with amazing efficiency. Complaints brought to me diminished, and often disappeared, even when the counselee did not fully understand the origin of the symptom or the purpose of the intervention.

Such was the case when a woman asked me for help with a recurring sleep problem. Several years before, she had successfully learned to manage a sleep problem. Recently her difficulty getting to sleep had returned. When people have solved problems in the past there is an excellent chance they can solve the problem again, usually very quickly. I tapped into her unused skill by giving her a motive to get to sleep. We agreed that she would go to bed as usual but if she was still awake after a half hour, she was to get one of her husband's theology texts and read for a full half hour after which she could try to sleep. She was to repeat this pattern until sleep overwhelmed her or morning broke, whichever came first. She reported back that she soon started sleeping right away and that it was no longer a problem.

Since it appears that humans are born to trouble, solving problems is something we do regularly. Pastors and other counselors are approached daily with questions and difficulties demanding some kind of assistance, and all too often they feel unable to counsel successfully in a short time period. Why is it that we cannot turn to the Bible and theology to find satisfying answers to all twentieth-century problems? One reason lies in the purpose of the Scriptures: they are to bring people to God for spiritual regeneration and life-renovating changes which prepare them for eternity in God's presence.

A second reason is found in the nature of biblical interpretation and theological formulations. God has made Himself known in two distinct ways: general and special revelation. When correctly understood, these two revelations are true, reliable, and integrated.

People communicate with each other on at least two channels: digital and analogical. Words are digital communication, and analogical communication includes all other information people convey to each other excluding the words they use. Consider which of these channels is most precise and easiest to interpret. Of course, digital (word) messages are easier to interpret than analogical ones, yet we spend three years in seminary learning how to translate, interpret, and preach the Scriptures, God's digital message. His analogical message is everything we find in creation and nature that serves as the subject of inquiry for scientists. Just as there are rules for interpreting the Bible so also are there rules for interpreting nature. Scientific method is a very slow and indefinite way of gaining information about people. It seems apparent that theologians' interpretation of the Bible and scientists' interpretation of nature are just that, interpretations—not the digital or analogical message itself. Putting it simply, the Word of God is infallible; biblical interpretations and scientific formulations are not. We need the Holy Spirit to properly understand general and special revelation and to correctly integrate the two distinct messages.

Integration is not the topic of this book. Yet the reader will observe from my use of biblical examples that much of what has been learned about counseling from the study of the general revelation is illustrated in the Bible.

This book introduces short-term counseling to students, pastors, professionals, and others involved in counseling. Some readers may conclude that short-term counseling is really only a set of procedures and methods, and this conclusion is partially true, for short-term counseling is practical. Yet it is not *only* common sense; short-term counseling contains elements of wisdom—the practical application of knowledge. Some of what is advanced here is easily discerned in the Scriptures; this "wisdom counseling" is found informally from the beginning of biblical history to its end, but only recently has it been formalized as a discipline within the field of modern psychotherapy.

THE ORGANIZATION OF THIS BOOK

Part 1 of this book reviews some counseling basics and theories that are fundamental to all counseling, but particularly to short-term counseling. In chapter 1, I attempt to give the reader an overview of short-term counseling, especially from the biblical perspective found in Exodus 18. General guidelines for making short-term interventions are introduced, as are the importance of the first contact and examples of what the counselor can expect as a result of counseling. Chapter 2 continues the overview by discussing the general nature of change as it occurs within as well as outside of the counseling context.

Chapter 3 looks at the nature of perception and reality. Just how much meaning do we place on the data as they are received through the sense gates? The answer to this question leads us to consider the adaptability of human perception. How does short-term counseling use this adaptability to facilitate change in the counselee's life?

What changes when counseling is successful is the topic of chapter 4. Various theoretical models are used to make sense of the unique successes of short-term counseling. Effective counseling requires a warm and accepting ambience allowing counselees to open their dreams and hurts to therapeutic scrutiny. Chapter 5 outlines the elements necessary for the swift development of that necessary caring relationship.

Part 2 shifts our attention to the stages through which the short-term counselor leads the counselee to change. In chapter 6 we undertake the crucial job of defining problems in such a way that solutions are evident. Getting at attempted solutions is the focus of chapter 7. As illustrated by the story of the woman with sleep problems, solutions are often already available to the counselee, and it is the counselor's job to unearth them and to put them to work again in the counselee's interest. Attempted solutions tell us something about how the counselee formulates the problem and what he or she is not willing to try again.

Chapter 8 helps the counselor establish with the counselee the goals of counseling. Without direction any project is doomed to failure, and counseling is no exception. Just establishing a goal may make the solution obvious.

Part 3 presents the major characteristics of short-term counseling: reframing and paradox. Chapter 9 introduces these unique interventions. Chapter 10 describes and illustrates reframing, which some have called the most elegant intervention, and chapter 11 tackles the confusing but powerful use of paradox. Specific and useful examples are suggested so the beginner can flesh out practical applications of short-term counseling. When understood and carefully applied, short-term counseling puts more tools in the counselor's kit, and readers may discover that short-term counseling is a curious and unfathomable resource for introducing effective changes into the lives of those they serve.

ACKNOWLEDGMENTS

Occasionally my wife and I attend a concert where we are delighted with the combined efforts of many musicians. *Short-*

Term Counseling is also a combined effort of many people to whom I am greatly indebted. Dennis Gibson introduced me to short-term counseling and served as a source of information and a sounding board in the early years of my romance with it. Without the help of Warren Heard, I would have missed the philosophical and theological implications of short-term principles. Steve Hungerford, Brad Zernov, Peter Neufeldt, and Dennis Humphrey carefully researched materials for several chapters. My editors, Tim Wise and Gary Collins, have patiently worked through the manuscript, making numerous corrections and helpful suggestions. Patient with the many years of reading and contemplation as well as the struggle to produce this manuscript has been my dear wife, Brenda, who for seemingly endless hours also edited and corrected errors. These people are my orchestra, and to them I doff my hat and say, *Thank you!*

PART ONE

The Basics

Chapter One

Short-Term Counseling and the Pastor

Once again the telephone rang in the middle of lunch. A woman (we'll call her Joan) was at the church asking to see me right away even though she had no appointment.

After quickly finishing lunch, I hurried to my office. There I encountered a disturbed middle-aged woman who was convinced that people could tell what she was thinking. Joan's story included an intimate relationship which followed the death of her husband. She explained her involvement and described a growing sense of guilt that eventually led her to end the affair. But to her surprise, out of anger she thought, the man had placed a listening device in her ear. Now he could tune in to what she was saying and sometimes even know what she thought.

Several doctors had assured Joan they could find no listening device and dismissed her as eccentric. When she came to me for help she was being seen by a psychiatrist who prescribed antipsychotic medications but was giving no further treatment. Desire for relief directed her to several therapists' offices; mine was next on her list. I counseled her for seven sessions, during which she talked less of the listening device than she did of intellectual, spiritual, and family interests. By the fifth or sixth session Joan and I began to realize that she was ready to get on with her life.

The principles and methods used in helping Joan provide the basis for this book. Short-term counseling techniques, in conjunction with medical treatment, assisted her in overcoming her painful symptoms. Although this case may seem unusual compared with the problems pastors or other counselors usually face, the principles and techniques used to promote Joan's recovery are practical and can be used in dealing with a variety of problems.

WHY THE PASTOR?

Since the early 1960s mental health care has been directed away from the large mental institutions and into local communities. But within these communities there are many who still need mental health care, including many of the homeless who wander urban streets and the strangers who come to our offices for help. Many seek this help from pastors.

Why is the pastor called on so frequently to counsel? Besides the growing need for counseling, pastors are readily AVAILABLE. Like Jesus, pastors constantly find themselves in the crush of the crowd, visible on Sunday morning, organizing and overseeing church programs, holding committee meetings, and visiting parishioners. People find it convenient to go to pastors because of this availability.

Still others turn to the pastor because society considers it RESPECTABLE. To consult with a minister for personal and family as well as spiritual problems does not have the negative implications that sometimes accompany going to a therapist. It embarrasses people to "hang out dirty laundry" in front of a stranger, and the pastor seems so friendly and safe.

Pastors are also AFFORDABLE. In the face of rising costs in mental health care, insurance companies are decreasing coverage for counseling services. Many people have nowhere else to turn but the church. Others cannot accept the idea of paying someone to listen. After all, isn't that what a *friend* does? Usually anyone looking for counsel from a pastor or professional counselor has already asked friends and relatives how to solve the problem. When these friends and relatives have not known how to help, the pastor is the next most likely person to ask.

WHY SHORT-TERM COUNSELING?

Short-term counseling provides a practical, powerful, effective, and efficient means of solving personal problems. Using short-term counseling means reduced counselee exposure, reduced time invested, reduced suffering, and effective problem solving.

REDUCED COUNSELEE EXPOSURE

Developing an effective pastoral counseling practice gets results, but it also creates a problem if the counselor is a pastor. Since some parishioners have difficulty staying in a church after they have let the pastor know so much about themselves, counseling does not necessarily build a larger congregation. Short-term counseling can minimize counselee exposure and help solve problems quickly. In a similar vein, successful short-term counseling may increase the counselor's client load since success tends to attract others in need.

REDUCED TIME INVESTED

Pressing public pressures may keep pastors from helping troubled people. This is especially true if the counseling process is going to take months or even years. When time is limited, counselors must decide what problems they will attempt to solve and how much time they can spend with any one person or family. With short-term counseling the pastor can conserve precious time for pressing congregational as well as community needs. The careful use of these powerful short-term counseling methods and principles can allow more people to recover in the same time period during which the pastor could formerly have counseled only a few.

REDUCED SUFFERING

Time concerns become critical when suffering is involved. The longer people suffer, the more discouragement and demoralization they experience. Time also ingrains the problem-engendering behavior. This, in many clients, makes change much more difficult. In addition, prolonged distress can lead to desperate attempts to escape pain, such as divorce, homicide, battering, and suicide. Stresses, too, can reduce the counselee's efficiency at work, in the home, and in the church.

Short-term therapy helps overcome these time-related problems. Coupled with early detection, short-term counseling limits how solidly the problem is established and helps the counselee regain courage and confidence, which influences how he or she approaches other problems in life. Short-term treatment addresses the client's essential needs and allows people to return to normal efficiency sooner, decreasing the extent of damage to social relationships. Time is strongly emphasized.

SOLVE PROBLEMS EFFECTIVELY

How does short-term counseling solve problems? Often the way the counselor and the counselee define a problem determines its solution. Difficult problems are often complicated because of the way they have been defined. The short-term approach redefines the problem in simple, solvable terms.

Since short-term counseling solves problems, it can be effective with a variety of social and emotional problems, and with people of all ages.[1] The age of the counselee does not preclude the use of short-term principles and methods. Young children respond remarkably well to environmental changes based on short-term interventions. Young and middle-aged adults can solve problems with a growing measure of wisdom and concern for getting on with life. Older persons can be helped to deal with life issues efficiently out of a need to conserve energy and resources. No pastoral counselor needs to avoid short-term counseling solely because of the apparent difficulty of a problem or the age of the counselee.

OVERVIEW OF SHORT-TERM COUNSELING

Short-term principles and methods may be understood within a four-part framework: (1) observe the problem, (2) plan a solution, (3) adjust the solution to the counselee, and (4) liberate the client to accept or reject the solution. It may help to remember that the first letters of each step spell OPAL. This pattern is illustrated in the problem-solving approach Jethro used in counseling Moses (Exod. 18:13–27).

OBSERVE THE PROBLEM

While visiting Moses' household Jethro observed how busy Moses was, working long days hearing and deciding legal cases presented by the people. Jethro noticed the negative effect of this heavy load. Perhaps Moses was showing signs of physical fatigue and distress. The stress might have been creating depression, irritablility, or anxiety. Somehow Jethro suspected that what Moses was doing was not good for him. None of these difficulties is recorded, but it is obvious that Jethro observed something in Moses' behavior that was dysfunctional. The older man gave Moses some wise counsel so he would not wear himself out.

Although the counselor does not usually approach people as Jethro did Moses, the helper needs to make careful observations of specific and concrete behaviors and their effects.[2] The counselor must look for words or behaviors or sense feelings that may give a clue about what the counselee is thinking.

PLAN THE SOLUTION

Once the problem has been observed, the next step is to plan the solution. This is done by looking at the coping solutions already at work in the person's life. The coping solutions looked at include attempts that proved inadequate, inappropriate, or inefficient, as well as those that work.

Coping Solutions. How do people get stuck in problems? In spite of reports by newspaper writers, TV news commentators, and local gossips that the whole world is filled with troubled people, on the whole most people function quite well. Living necessarily involves continuous problem solving. Many troubled people have only recently encountered a problem they could not solve. So how do we explain the problems that individuals seem unable to solve?

When people face novel situations that call for some kind of solution-oriented behavior, they try to cope with the present problem as they dealt with similar situations in the past. This process is the basis of coping behavior. If an old solution works with the new problem the issue is solved. If it doesn't work, the problem solver will try again, usually attempting a similar solution or a repetition of some earlier approach.

Inefficient Solutions. Sometimes the "solution" itself becomes a new problem. While walking to work one morning, Susan had an unexpected fainting spell that severely frightened her. She immediately stepped into a nearby store and sat down. Her fainting feeling decreased and she continued on to work. The next morning, to avoid the location of the fearful fainting spell and the possibility of a repetition, she took the bus to work. Susan's safety zone continued to narrow until several years later her anxiety was so severe that she rarely left her home. When she did go out, it was only in company with another person. One morning when her children were small, she discovered that her son had wandered into the street. But her fear was so great that she would not leave her home to get him out of danger! Her reaction to an unexplained fainting spell had triggered solutions directed at avoiding fearful places even in times of emergency.

Susan was stuck because she was applying her solution, which was avoidance, to a problem that could only be solved by being faced. Sometimes people, like this lady, give up trying to solve the problem and choose instead to live with it. This kind of reaction may result when a person is unable to solve a problem, even after trying repeatedly, so the problem solver concludes that no solution exists. Others do not even try because they are so overwhelmed with the new problem that they do not believe a solution could possibly exist.

Undoubtedly Moses applied problem-solving experiences he had used earlier in his life to settle the disputes of the Israelites. During his forty-year exile from Egypt, he was a captain in Jethro's family. His duties, no doubt, included the mediation of disputes in his own household. His method of managing his personal household was probably similar to the way he attempted to govern the house of Israel. But the system was not efficient when the population was multiplied by millions and the number of disputes by the hundreds. Moses' solution was not wrong; it was just inefficient. This inefficiency is what Jethro observed as he watched a fatigued and overwhelmed Moses attempt to meet the needs of millions of Israelites.

Adequate Solutions.   Gordon and Meyers-Anderson, drawing on the therapeutic techniques of noted psychiatrist and psychotherapist Milton H. Erickson, use flexibility, humor, and future orientation to help people construct adequate solutions for their problems.[3] By the time the client comes for counsel, *flexibility* in solving the problem has disappeared. The flexible client must be able to view the problem situation from different perspectives. Often clients only see the difficulty in one way and may have concluded that it cannot be solved. A counselor's use of *humor*, often injects the situation with objectivity, and the problem is put into a different light. A *future orientation* allows the counselee to look away from the immediate situation, which has been identified as unsolvable, and to think what life would be like without the problem. This future-oriented perspective often lets the counselee see what needs changing in order to arrive at the desired state.

Adjust the Solution

If people are going to change, they need to see how the problem and the solution are connected. Understanding how a person views the world in general and the problem in particular opens the way to discovering this connection. The effective counselor attempts to understand the counselee's world view.[4] The counselee's use of solutions in other settings may give clues to possible solutions for a current problem.

Some attempts to help fail, however, because the proposed solution does not fit the person's understanding of the problem. Jethro did not make this mistake. Instead, he followed his observations with a suggestion that allowed Moses to fulfill his God-ordained responsibility. Jethro resolved the problem within Moses' understanding of how he was commissioned by God to relate to the Israelites. If the suggestion had been outside of that understanding, Jethro's attempt would probably have failed. By teaching the people the Word of God and choosing under-judges, Moses could fulfill his responsibility. Jethro was expertly handling short-term techniques.

Unlike Jethro, sometimes the modern counselor fails when adapting the suggestion to the person's way of thinking. When this happens the counselor's suggestions are resisted, perhaps for weeks or months. In contrast, if the counselor tailors the suggestion to make sense within the person's outlook, the idea is likely to be accepted with little, if any, question.

Recently, a graduate student we'll call Mike agreed to present a personal problem in front of one of my counseling classes. Mike described his problem as becoming very frightened and withdrawn when an authority figure disagreed with him. This reaction was troublesome because he often made presentations to college and university presidents, who fit perfectly his idea of authority figures. Mike was committed to making the presentations but felt very uncomfortable. Whenever Mike faced such situations he usually withdrew. This withdrawal gave me a clue as to how I needed to adjust my solution so that he would accept it. I told Mike he was not withdrawing very effectively and suggested that he withdraw by letting the authority figure know that he was concerned about objections that might be raised and that he wanted them written down so he could prepare answers. He could do this after the meeting if he did not know the answer when the questions were raised, and call or write back. This suggestion fit him so well that he readily accepted it. Now he has new confidence because he has a different way to meet his personal need and still perform his responsibility.

LIBERATE THE CLIENT

Even though the counselor carefully observes the problem and plans and adjusts the solution to the client's perspective, the counseling effort can still fail if action does not follow.[5] In our Old Testament example, the previous relationship between Jethro and Moses could have hindered the counseling effort. Moses was Jethro's son-in-law and had been a member of his household for forty years. However, as an advisor Jethro made a proposal and allowed Moses to consider the suggestion under God's authority. Jethro's suggestion was within Moses' understanding of what God wanted him to do.

Some counselors may find it difficult to switch from the role of prophet to the role of counselor. Pastoral counselors are especially inclined to keep people from experiencing problems by telling them what to do. Instead, we must help people understand biblical truth and then guide them into obedience. Coercion is not shepherding. We must always lead the sheep, not drive them.

Presenting the suggestion tentatively increases the likelihood of people acting on it because we have not violated their personal independence. Respecting personal independence also increases the probability that the client will take responsibility for the results. If the results are not desirable, the counselor can address the problem again, possibly with increased client motivation. If the results are acceptable, then the counselee is able to feel encouraged about making a change that produces a better situation.

Jethro successfully counseled Moses, who adopted the solution by instituting a judicial system to handle the myriad of problems generated by millions of people on the move. Part of Jethro's success was the wisdom of the suggestion that he carefully presented to Moses. We need to emulate Jethro by approaching those we must help with the same kind of wisdom and diplomacy.

THE IMPORTANCE OF THE FIRST CONTACT

Most people find it difficult to ask for help. By the time they make the first contact, a great deal of tension has built up over the problem. Learning what triggered the call for help can assist the counselor in making an early intervention. As discussed before, people who come for counseling have usually already tried a number of things, albeit inconsistently or ineffectively, to solve the problem on their own. An early intervention can often be built on the foundation of these previous attempts made.

Many people approach counseling with fear. The counselor can help allay this fear by genuinely accepting their concerns and letting them know they are not unusual. On occasion I compare counseling with going to school. I suggest, "If you wanted to learn how to take better photographs or how to sew, you would probably look for an expert or take a course in a local school." They usually respond by agreeing with this course of action. I then point out how counseling is a one-on-one learning experience resulting in the more effective handling of some kinds of life experiences. Generally the first contact lets counselors help normalize the experience for those who are fearful or hesitant.

EVALUATING THE NEED

People who make the first request for help come with varying levels of need. The counselor should evaluate that need before making the initial appointment. Generally people can wait, but occasionally someone has a crisis underway and immediate attention is indicated. In such cases the verbal request is supported by the tone and quality of the voice backing up the verbal message. In order to assess people's needs, learn to listen not only to the words but to how the words are said.

Depression can present a critical need that must be evaluated to determine how soon the person needs to be seen. People who sound depressed should be questioned regarding the length of time of this depression and whether they live alone or have other support people in their lives. People who are alone and sound seriously depressed rank high on the priority list. You probably should see this person immediately, unless you *know* their depression and subsequent call for help is a pattern of manipulating people. On one occasion such a manipulative person called me for help, and I involved the police who went immediately to check on her need. This radical move demonstrated my concern and intention to protect her life, even though she did not appreciate it.

SETTING LIMITS

As early as possible, try to give some details regarding place and time. The latter is especially important for the pastoral counselor because people know that pastors schedule their own appointments and study times, and, therefore, counselees often think the pastoral counselor can devote several hours to helping them. Providing them with a beginning *and* ending time for the appointment lets them know you expect to move on to other duties by a specified time. For people who insist on violating time constraints, counselors wisely schedule another client for the following hour so they are forced to excuse themselves when the allotted time ends.

ESTABLISHING A PLACE

Place is another parameter established by the counselor. Generally it is best to counsel in a place of the counselor's choosing rather than in the home or elsewhere, except where obvious needs for other considerations exist. Pastoral counseling is generally separated from pastoral care on the basis of a specific place for counseling and a set time. Anything else is considered general care and provided for all members and friends of the church.

Furthermore, the setting for counseling must be a place where there can be confidentiality, ruling out any chance of voices carrying to an adjoining room. Windows should be covered so people cannot see into the office where they might recognize the counselee. Decorations should be quiet and restful, using soft tones, appropriate draperies, tasteful pictures, and other necessary appointments. Desk tops should be obscured or very neat, since a messy or cluttered desk distracts people and gives the impression that they are keeping you from other important business.

In the ideal setting the counselor has a separate office, furnished and appointed much like a living room, for counseling and other informal meetings. A special counseling office removes the counselor from the routine matters of life but allows control over the environment and keeps the clutter of a busy life out of view.

THE RESULTS OF CHRISTIAN COUNSELING

What can a counselor expect when people have been helped by counseling? A danger lies in the mythological goal of perfection held by many people. The Christian faith *seems* to teach perfection, and the counselor, like many other highly educated people, is subject to perfectionistic thinking. Perfection is not an attainable goal. However, there are at least four ways that counselees will likely improve as the result of specifically Christian counseling: increased courage, increased effectiveness, increased social interest, and increased spirituality.

INCREASED COURAGE

With increased courage people begin to move toward life rather than away from it. Life takes on a new zest, and people are more able to take advantage of opportunities that come their way. Alfred Adler's theory of psychotherapy classified troubled people as *dis*couraged rather than mentally sick. Short-term counseling generates courage because, from the beginning, people learn that their problems are not so unusual and they are able to make at least small improvements in their situations.

Such a change is illustrated in the experience of a woman who bit her nails to the extent her nails were painful and the problem was obvious to anyone who knew her. She considered her nail biting habit unsightly; and although she had tried repeatedly to quit, success had remained elusive. I asked her to keep a record of her nail biting habit including where, when, and under what conditions she bit her nails. At the end of the week she reported that the assignment was difficult, but she noted that she bit her nails far less than before. I urged her to try harder at getting a detailed record, but the result was less biting. At the third interview, I told her she had to decide whether she really wanted to quit biting her nails. Perhaps the biting had some important tension-relieving value to her and she should consider carefully for several days the question of continuing. She came back with a firm decision to quit altogether, which she did.

INCREASED EFFECTIVENESS

When people win these kinds of victories, they feel better about themselves, and this changes their outlook on life. Solving one problem encourages them to try solving others, and the chain of success leads them into more and more victories. If they run into a problem that gives them trouble, they know they can turn to experts to help them solve it.

Job observed, "Yet man is born to trouble as surely as sparks fly upward" (Job 5:7). Psychologists observe that people need at least some tension to keep life interesting and challenging. People who benefit from counseling are not perfected but prepared to meet the challenges of life, if not with a complete set of new tools, then with the conviction that they *can* find solutions for life's problems.

INCREASED SOCIAL INTEREST

Troubled people focus on themselves. This natural result of experiencing pain keeps them from taking into account other people's needs, and this can alienate even the closest of friends. As individuals begin to recover, their interests turn outward to include other people, an ameliorated situation that encourages counselees and promotes their further growth. In some cases people with problems actually cling to others in an unhealthy way. Clinging people, however, are really intensely focused on themselves even though they may appear very sociable. Healthy individuals are able to take the needs and wishes of others into account along with their own and not be threatened. Healthy people are balanced socially.

INCREASED SPIRITUALITY

Similarly, healthy people can focus on God rather than on earthly matters, especially their own concerns. They begin to take on the character of Christ because they are now able to put aside other concerns and learn about Him, a process that increases their knowledge and concomitant obedience. The woman who thought she had a listening device in her ear soon began to develop social interests and began to take renewed interest in prayer, Bible reading, and fellowship with other Christians. Not until her problem was mending did she consider herself acceptable to God—an accomplished fact in Christ's death, but an unreality to her. The reality of forgiveness took root and flourished when she could free herself from the torment of guilt and unrealistic thinking.

FINALLY

This chapter provides an overview of short-term counseling. The theoretical and practical landscape before us merely begins to summarize and explore the possibilities open to the reader who will read, apply, and explore still further the offerings of other theorists and authors. We want to peak your therapeutic interest by salting the palate of your mind with just a sampling of the creative short-term materials available. *Bon appetit!*

NOTES

1. A survey of the literature on short-term counseling illustrates its use with various ages across a variety of problems. The early studies of the Mental Research Institute focused on schizophrenia among young adults but evolved into a study of communication patterns within the family. Milton H. Erickson demonstrated the use of short-term techniques with children as well as adults.

2. R. Dayringer, *The Heart of Pastoral Counseling: Healing through relationship* (Grand Rapids, Mich.: Zondervan, 1989), 26–30.

3. D. Gordon and M. Meyers-Anderson, *Phoenix: Therapeutic patterns of Milton H. Erickson* (Cupertino, Calif.: Meta Publications, 1981), 27–33.

4. Gerard Egan, *The Skilled Helper: A systematic approach to effective helping,* 4th ed. (Pacific Grove, Calif.: Brooks/Cole, 1990), 125.

5. Egan, *The Skilled Helper,* 85.

Chapter Two

The Components of Change

"YES, JOHN, DID YOU HAVE SOME COMMENT to make to the class?"

"Well . . . I don't think Hawthorne could have meant all we have seen in this story," replied John.

"Perhaps he didn't," answered the teacher, "but we are discovering the power of words to mean many things to different people."[1]

James (3:1–12) warned about the power of words in his description of the destructiveness of the tongue. Scripture repeatedly illustrates God's powerful but positive use of words. When "in the beginning" God spoke the creation into existence, words linked His creativity and power to produce immense output. With words Nathan constructed a net in which David caught himself (2 Sam. 12:1–10) and out of which he started a renewed relationship with God. Timothy (2 Tim. 3:16–17) calculated the power of God's Word to change the life of anyone who is instructed by it. It is interesting to observe how changes came about in the lives of biblical characters and how change occurs in general. In chapter 1 we looked at change from the counselor's point of view, but here we consider change from the counselee's perspective.

CONTRAST

At least three ingredients are essential for change to occur. The first of these is contrast. Contrast arouses attention and shows us the need for change. Human beings are continuously bombarded by stimuli. Paying attention to all the available information is impossible. Through a process called deselection, we cope by selecting only some of the stimuli available to us at any given moment.

Consider the importance of deselection in learning to drive a car. If we could not ignore irrelevant stimuli, such as the song on the radio, and focus on the relevant stimuli, such as steering, speed, and objects in the road, we would become like the proverbial centipede who wondered which leg came after the other and ended in the ditch. Most sensory input must be ignored in order to focus on essential driving behaviors. Our attention is drawn to deselected stimuli when what we perceive does not match what we expect to happen. This contrast arrests and fixes our attention until we understand and control the new pattern, and then the deselection process starts again.

The Old Testament abounds with evidence of God's ability to use contrast to get attention. God gave people freedom of choice and granted human beings limited sovereignty. In so doing, He committed Himself to work with human will by approaching people through their understanding. This makes securing attention part of God's commitment to respect the autonomy of His creatures. This contrast may come in the form of shock, or it may be more subtle.

SHOCK

Nathan's approach to David illustrates using shock to get someone's attention. After he committed adultery with Bathsheba and had Uriah killed, David returned to his daily activities. To what extent his life was affected by what he had done is uncertain; it is clear, however, that God wanted to deal with David's sin. In order to do so He needed David's attention, and so He sent Nathan with a story designed to shock him into facing his sinful actions.

When Nathan told David the story of the rich man who stole the poor man's lamb, David's anger was aroused against such a person. Yet David could not see that his crime matched the rich man's treachery in Nathan's story. What a stunning blow Nathan delivered when he said, "You are the man." He had David's attention!

God also used shock to get Moses' attention (Exodus 3–4). Forty years had passed since he killed the Egyptian, and Moses, no doubt, was not even thinking about his original desire or his vain attempt to rescue his people from slavery. With the burning bush, God attracted Moses' attention so that He could communicate with him. Why the burning bush? Could not God have simply spoken to Moses anywhere? Moses needed to be prepared by being attentive to what God would say to him. The holiness and sovereignty of God were part of the message Moses needed to comprehend. So, in the form of a fire that did not destroy the bush (an interesting message in itself), God captured Moses' attention.

What thoughts did Isaiah have just before God shocked him with the temple vision (Isaiah 6)? He may have been concerned about some mundane matter, some future plan, or some pensive recollection about King Uzziah. Did Isaiah think, *Today I will hear from God?* It is not that Isaiah looked for God but that God looked for Isaiah. God arrested his attention in the vision, and only then was Isaiah prepared to make a significant life-changing decision.

Shock was part of God's approach even with people who welcomed a message from Him. Ezekiel was wandering in the fields when God surprised him into attentiveness with a mystifying vision of His throne (Ezekiel 1). Daniel was shaken physically and troubled cognitively by a vision where God disclosed centuries of political prophecy (Daniel 7). And God shockingly spoke to Belshazzar in a mysterious message written on a wall (Daniel 5).

The Old Testament has no monopoly on the use of shock to fix attention. Jesus used surprise just as effectively as did His heavenly Father. For example, the startling way Jesus replied to Nicodemus drew him into a life-changing conversation (John 3:3). After gaining his attention, Jesus proceeded with a dialogue that changed Nicodemus's thinking. Consider also how the woman of Sychar was surprised by a Jew who asked her, a Samaritan, for a drink of water (John 4). Jesus used the cultural barrier between them to start a process of change that transformed her life and the lives of her neighbors and friends.

Jesus arranged a situation to teach His disciples a lesson and to do good for a blind man. The act of applying a homemade medicine drew attention to what Jesus was doing, and the obvious result was arrested attention and a changed life (John 9).

SUBTLETY

Shock and surprise are not the only ways to get attention. God can speak subtly. The contrasting whisper in the midst of the violent wind and the earthquake spoke to Elijah (1 Kings 19:12). God also convinced Abraham to deepen his trust and commitment by giving him a severe test. Abraham obediently prepared for the trip to Moriah where, in obedience to God, he would offer Isaac on the altar (Genesis 22). Was this a message of confidence? The ram God provided was a quiet but concrete message that challenged and completed Abraham's faith in the God who never fails.

Doing nothing can also draw attention. Note how Jesus focused the attention of the accusers of the woman taken in adultery (John 8). By simply waiting and writing on the ground, the accusers were challenged to focus on what Jesus was going to do. This concentration opened them to receive and learn from the paradoxical message Jesus delivered.[2]

COGNITION

The second ingredient essential for change is cognition. Cognition involves processing information and thoughts. The client needs to understand the problem and its solution in order to change. This understanding encompasses the reasoning process, the information itself, and the client's beliefs and perceptions. The means a counselor employs to arrest the attention of a client can effectively force the counselee to face the problem. Change involves not only getting attention but also facilitating change.

REASONING

"Cognition refers to the symbolic or mental processes of human beings engaged in thinking, reasoning, creating, and solving problems."[3] It begins with developing consciousness or awareness and involves conscious considerations of what needs to be done. This contemplation of actions means the individual is thinking objectively; he or she is reasoning.

Even though God had judged King David for his sin, the effectiveness of that verdict to bring about change in him was yet to be experienced. Nathan opened David's mind to what he had done by helping him get an objective view of the crime. Only by seeing, through Nathan's story, what the sin would look like in the life of another person could David get beyond the defense he had established as a result of his sin. This story not only got David's attention, it helped David understand. Both attention and cognition resulted from this same incident. Both are distinct and important and can require distinct operations to achieve.

INFORMATION

Short-term counseling helps people sift out what can be changed and the attitudes and perceptions which usually keep people from finding successful solutions.[4] The quality of this sifting is directly related to the precision of the thought process and the accuracy of information. People do make decisions based on false information.

Consider some biblical examples. In Genesis 3, Eve operates on the basis of accurate information until she is confronted with the serpent's doubt-engendering challenge. The cornerstone of the Devil's attack was to question the accuracy of the information God had given her through Adam. If the Devil's question is given credence, Eve's consequent behavior makes cognitive sense, even though it denies reality.

Gideon based his attack on the Midianite camp on the confusion of the Midianites' cognitive processes (Judges 7). Indeed, God worked on behalf of Gideon, but it was also God who told Gideon how to approach and defeat the Midianites—use trumpets, pitchers, and torches to destroy the enemy. The rout took place first in the minds of the enemy because the facts, if they had been known, would not have supported their confusion and subsequent self-imposed defeat. The Midianites acted on inaccurate information.

The caution that characterized Gideon's acceptance of God's assignment gives an interesting contrast to the Midianite fiasco (Judg. 6:36–40). Gideon needed to be convinced of the fact that God was behind the plan to rescue Israel. Therefore, he asked God twice to wet the fleece or ground as verification. And God recognized Gideon's need for certainty when He sent him to the Midianite camp to spy on them. These biblical examples are not exhaustive, but they are illustrative of how information plays an effective role in cognitive processing.

BELIEFS

A belief is the result of the natural process of sorting and associating stimuli. We are continuously assaulted by stimuli; and in order to function, we must deselect information. The organization of stimuli into patterns is a necessary function of the human brain. These patterns consist of bits of similar information which coalesce into thoughts about ourselves and our environment. We experience, theorize, and verify what we are concluding about the environment. These conclusions are actually generic beliefs. All subsequent stimuli are interpreted on the basis of earlier beliefs.[5] Short-term counseling assists the client in sorting and associating stimuli resulting in an acceptable belief pattern rather than misusing the information with a resulting belief in an erroneous conclusion.

When Gideon's attack broke out and the rout started, the Midianites believed they were being attacked by a large army. Their consternation defeated them. Note, too, how God told Joshua to set an ambush for the army of Ai (Josh. 8:1–2). The leaders of Ai believed they would defeat the Israelites as they had done before. On the basis of that belief, the army of Ai followed the army of Israel in the retreat only to find they had been tricked. In this case the information Ai received was accurate—the Israelites were retreating—but it was not the whole Israeli army. Ai was defeated not by what its army saw but by what the soldiers believed was happening.

Goliath's fatal error, too, was not in what he saw before him but in what he believed about what he saw. Here was just a boy, and who was a boy in a battle with the giant? After all, had not the whole Israeli army and the king allowed this giant to bully and terrify them for forty days before David arrived? Perhaps Israel's fear had stimulated the giant to an overconfidence that led him fatally to underestimate what a boy, a boy who is backed by God, can do. Goliath was killed because of what he believed about what he saw.

PERCEPTION

Human perception organizes and elaborates sensations into meaningful wholes. Our senses provide the input data which, when processed through the reasoning facilities of the mind, present us with conclusions or perceptions of our world. The result is experiencing the world around us.[6] As you are aware, information and belief are closely related and closely associated with perception. As we have seen, beliefs influence perceptions. Goliath believed himself invincibly strong; and because of what he believed and the influence it had on his perception, he discounted the situation before him.

Parables challenge our perception of reality, and a well-placed parable can be an avenue to force the client to face a mistaken perception. "A carefully crafted story can be an ideal way to get behind someone's defenses when a merely abstract argument could be easily parried in the cut and thrust of debate."[7] How does the parable insinuate its message? Besides the element of surprise or contrast that arrests the attention of the hearers, the parable arouses curiosity and draws the listener into the process of thinking about what was said. The puzzling aspect of the parable forces the listeners to rethink their position, and by doing so they have the opportunity to revise beliefs and assumptions because they have temporarily adopted a different perspective. The parable helps to generate an objective viewpoint.

Consider the impact of Jesus' story about the sower and the seed (Matthew 13) and its impact on the perceptions of those who listened. Some of them may have wondered, "What's this man getting at?" They knew His reputation and so expected some wisdom from Him. Instead He spoke cryptically of sowing and seed. Their perception, a combination of their expectations incited by Jesus' reputation and the mystery surrounding His remarks, challenged them to a new level of cognitive processing. This is another example of contrast drawing attention. With aroused curiosity the listeners had more opportunity to be open to what Jesus said than if He had attempted to tell them straight out.

Jesus seems to uncover this strategy in His explanation to the disciples. In quoting Isaiah, Jesus hinted what He knew of their innermost thoughts. "Hearing but never understanding" and "seeing but never perceiving" describe a closed and narrow person (Matthew 13:14). With defenses in place, conclusions formed, and beliefs established, people are walled in with old ways of thinking and behaving and walled out from new ideas or the truth. Getting through the psychological wall is what the parable accomplishes so well, for it slips through defenses and deposits a message that must be considered.

The parable leads the listener into new territories of knowledge and understanding by starting with the familiar (e.g., seeds, soils, weeds, treasures, pearls, nets). Learning proceeds by taking the learner from the known to the unknown. If we can take something the client already knows, believes, and understands and demonstrate how a new idea relates to it, then learning takes place more easily and quickly.

A simile, a comparison which can take the listener from the known to the unknown, can also influence perception. "The kingdom of heaven is like . . ." signals the Lord's effort to disclose the incomprehensible characteristics of heaven in familiar terms (See Matt. 13:24, 31, 44 for examples). Many of the Old Testament prophets were left speechless when they tried to describe what God had revealed of Himself to them. And in the New Testament, even John, who knew Jesus so well, was limited to describing his glorious Lord with terms "like a son of man," only vaguely giving the reader a glimpse of Jesus' glory (Rev. 1:13). For centuries poets have attempted to draw their readers into greater understanding of life, love, and death by using the familiar to explain the unfamiliar. In many ways all of us struggle daily to put into language the original thoughts generated in our minds.

The efforts church committees expend in putting policy into writing is another example of how difficult it is to put thought into language. A church I served decided to put into writing its missionary policies. Several meetings were devoted to clarifying policies and writing the actual manual that would be presented to the congregation. When the manual was completed, several meetings and considerable discussion were required to help the people understand what was intended in the policy statements. Even though the policies were carefully worded, many people still had difficulty in understanding what was meant. Similar confusion exists in many corporate offices and faculty committee meetings.

People need stability. The human mind is full of information that has been categorized and combined into conclusions and beliefs which influence perception. Our need for stability means we tend to reject new information or ideas. We often ignore what we are plainly told but accept what we have come to conclude on our own. The parable avoids this inclination by allowing the listener to determine the meaning. The mystery in the parable not only arouses attention, it leaves room for conclusion and ownership. Ownership ensures that the listener will not easily give up what has been learned.[8]

CORRECTION

So far, we have considered two aspects of change as illustrated in the lives of biblical characters. The first was the importance of contrast to gain attention; the second was cognition, which involves processing of information and thoughts. Just as fuel and oxygen are necessary for a fire to start, change requires attention, thought, and then correction. James echoed this triad when he said,

Do not merely listen to the word, and so deceive yourselves. Do what it says. Anyone who listens to the word but does not do what it says is like a man who looks at his face in a mirror and, after looking at himself, goes away and immediately forgets what he looks like. (James 1:22–24)

In this passage attention is assumed, and because some thought process must accompany self-deception, cognitive processing is implied between the first two clauses. What James highlights in this admonition is the correction process. The simple analogy about looking into the mirror and doing nothing about what is seen underscores the sensibility of change. The obvious truth of the analogy creeps through the reader's defenses and supports the wisdom of seriously considering what God says by making appropriate changes. The man who is blessed looks intently into God's Word and does what he sees written there.

MOTIVATION

Correction begins with motivation. Because God has given people freedom of choice and has committed Himself to working with the thinking processes, He must also deal with people's motivation. Motivation occurs when an individual experiences a face-to-face confrontation with an actual or perceived need.[9] Motivation can develop out of spiritual, physiological, or psychological (cognitive) needs. While little empirical study has been devoted to spiritual motivation, considerable animal research has focused on physiological motivation which can be defined as hunger, thirst, and sex.[10] Festinger formulated a now-popular theory explaining cognitive motivation.[11] People are uncomfortable when what they think of the world and themselves does not match reality. The effort to relieve this tension can change behavior or thinking and is defined as cognitive motivation.

Most preaching attempts to create this tension by helping the listeners recognize the difference between what they are and what God wants them to be. The resulting spiritual motivation is based first on cognitive tension (Rom. 10:17). Jesus fostered the Samaritan woman's motivation by creating tension between what she understood and what He said to her (John 4:4–42). Beginning with "everyone who drinks this water will be thirsty again," a fact that fit with her understanding of herself and the world, He created tension with the next statement: "but whoever drinks the water I give him will never thirst. Indeed, the water I give him will become in him a spring of water welling up to eternal life." The immediate response betrays her motivation: "Sir, give me this water so that I won't get thirsty and have to keep coming here to draw water." Jesus had created a cognitive motivation in order to develop a spiritual motivation later, for He spoke both of natural and supernatural water. The woman first recognized the natural water but later became aware of the supernatural need she had and the provision this Man was able to supply.

A comparable trend can be seen in how, over centuries, God dealt with the Israelites. They followed a pattern of moving toward Him and then moving away. When He wanted them to learn a spiritual lesson, God deprived them of even the necessities of life resulting in a high level of physical and cognitive motivation. Then they were ready to concentrate on their spiritual relationship with Him. One motivation can lead to another.

Encouraging motivation is critical in any learning situation, and curiosity is one important method of encouraging motivation. "We experience our strongest motivation in those situations that are puzzling."[12] When all the facts are plainly laid out and the listener has nothing to figure out, the motivation level drops significantly. Leaving something for the listener to figure out raises the motivation level.

PLANNING

Motivation is also related to experiences of success. When people understand what should happen next, they can better judge how far they have come in solving the problem. Establishing a goal and breaking down the path to the goal into achievable steps allows for a feeling of accomplishment. Several psychological systems contribute similar principles for developing a workable plan.

Flexible. One of the problems common to most people who seek counseling is the limited nature of their choices. Typically they have tried to solve their problems by using existing coping skills, and when these fail they often turn to friends, relatives, and neighbors for advice. When all of these sources fail to help them out of their predicament, they usually feel as though their problems have no answers. Therefore, the counselor must remain objective and use problem-solving skills to assist counselees in finding additional ways to relieve their stress. Building alternatives into the counseling plan gives counselees renewed hope because now they have new ideas to counteract their belief that no solutions exist. Alternatives also allow the counselees to choose among several options.

When the rich young ruler approached Jesus, he had only one option in mind for answering his question about eternal certainty (Matt. 19:16–22). When Jesus hit on that one option, he could answer firmly that he had kept all the commandments from childhood. However, Jesus gave him another alternative that touched on his real need. He appeared to cling to his wealth, and this clinging kept him from freely giving to his fellow men. The second option offered by Jesus gave him a new way out, even though he did not seem to be able to take it that day.

Observable. The second part of Jesus' counsel to the rich young ruler illustrates the next important point in planning. Jesus counseled him to go and sell all that he had and give to the poor. Although unacceptable, the solution was concrete. Vague solutions almost certainly end in failure. People need to know that they are getting something accomplished relative to their problem. If the plan is vague, progress could exist but not be measurable, and the client would become discouraged unnecessarily. Vague steps in the plan must be converted into concrete ones. For example, a goal of loving a spouse more is good but not observable. Converting this goal can be accomplished by asking, "What would be happening if you were more loving to your spouse than you are now?" More will be said about this later in chapter 8 on setting goals.

Repeatable. Consider the importance of repetition in problem solving. The old saying, practice makes perfect, is true if the practice is correct. Habits are not easily broken, but they are breakable. Repeatable behavior is important to establishing a new habit pattern. Once we choose a new behavior to solve a problem, the frequency of repetition determines the success of the outcome. Besides, if something happens so rarely that it cannot be frequently repeated, it likely will have little effect on the problem.

In Ephesians (4:20–32) Paul speaks first of the total change to the inner, spiritual person, which demonstrates itself in a transformed psychological attitude. These changes must activate a change in behavior, and Paul proceeds to outline this change. Note the general thrust of his counsel: putting off completely and putting on repeatedly. First Paul calls for putting off lying and replacing such behavior with telling the truth. It is not enough to stop doing wrong; right behavior must take the place of what was wrong. He illustrates the same concept in the exhortation to replace stealing with giving, and filthy conversation with helpful talk. The changed behavior is repeated. Paul's counsel calls for changes (telling the truth, giving to the poor, etc.) that by their nature repeat. Paul knows the new man will build righteous habits to replace the evil ones formed when the old nature was in control.

Limitable.   The counseling plan needs to help the client understand the time-limited nature of the change. This is not a contradiction of the repeatable nature of change but is, rather, a look at the change from the client's perspective. Making a commitment for a lifetime or for a vague period of time can keep counselees from making the changes at all. Notice how Daniel (1:6–20) convinced the doubting Ashpenaz to change the young Israelites' diets for a limited time in order to prove the correctness of the decision. Ashpenaz was willing to make a time-limited commitment whereas it is unlikely he would have changed their diets otherwise; and, of course, the plan of action proved very wise and healthy. Their good health encouraged Ashpenaz to continue the dietary restrictions of these four young men.

COMMITMENT

Naaman illustrates the importance of commitment (2 Kings 5). If Naaman had not washed in the Jordan as instructed, he would not have been healed. The way Elisha handled Naaman cured two problems: the obvious one was his leprosy, but the prophet also challenged Naaman's pride, a problem more serious than leprosy (Daniel 4). Pride sets up a serious obstacle to change because it keeps us from trying new solutions. Yet pride is not the only barrier to change. The rich young ruler presumably did not change because of his dependence on his wealth. After his rooftop vision, Peter could have refused to change based on tradition (Acts 10:9–23). So whether the obstacle to change is pride, dependence, or tradition, commitment to change is the last link in the process of solving problems.

So far we have only examined briefly three examples of handling commitment. Now let's note how God the Father promoted commitment to bring about life-change. Moses was not considering change when God spoke to him from the burning bush. As pointed out earlier, God needed to get his attention and give him new information, but He needed also to get Moses going. Basically God needed to overcome Moses' objections.

First, Moses objected on the basis of who he was, and God answered by saying, "I will be with you" (Exod. 3:12). In essence Moses cried out, "I'm a nobody," and God responded with "I'm somebody and they'll pay attention to Me." Commitment often hinges on the proximity of the helper. Moses needed God to be near him and so does the person who is changing behavior. Behavioral change is difficult, and a close relationship to the helper is important.

That was all Moses really needed to get the job done, but his objections go on to question God's identity: "Who are you?" In answer, God gave Moses the authoritative word: "I AM has sent me" (3:14). Commitment to change can take place easier when the counselee believes in the ability of the counselor to understand. When counselees are not able to believe in themselves, they can borrow from the counselor until new behaviors yield changes that are pleasing and therefore reinforcing.

Then Moses raised the question of the Israelites' disbelief (4:1) for which God gave him a series of certifying signs. This part of the text may not seem to fit the counseling situation until you consider all the people the counselee must convince that some change has taken place. Of course, we cannot give them miraculous signs to perform, but we can help them believe in the effectiveness of what they are going to do. This belief helps them move into change with greater confidence.

Moses may have been the first "yes, but" client ever recorded, for he raised another objection for God to answer. This last protest centered on his physical disability which God tried to disregard. Moses insisted, and God gave him Aaron as his assistant. No question about it, Moses' obstinacy irritated God, but He relented and provided human companionship. This part of the story illustrates another important aid in getting people to change: get them connected with people who will encourage and stimulate their growth. Companionship divides the burden and promotes commitment.

Change is part of everyone's life, but channeling change into growth is paramount in counseling.[13] Because people have the freedom of choice, we, like God, must work with them and not try to force their will. We must get their attention so that they can receive new or correct information for cognitive processing. Finally we need to help them convert what they learn into new behaviors that become self-reinforcing. Once they try and succeed, they are more likely to follow a new course. Even God the Father and the Lord Jesus Christ used such procedures and techniques to promote healthy change in the lives of biblical characters. By Their example They challenge us to become better biblical counselors.

NOTES

1. Jay Efran, M. Lukens, and R. Lukens, *Language, Structure, and Change: Frameworks of meaning in psychotherapy* (New York: Norton, 1990), 29.

2. Note also the subtle approach used by Abraham's servant in finding God's choice of a wife for Isaac (Genesis 24); the quiet means by which God provided a lifesaving supply of oil for a widow (1 Kings 17; 2 Kings 4); Jesus' casual interview with the rich young ruler (Luke 18:18–29); and the multitude of examples of how God arrested the attentions of the great and lowly, the foolish and wise, and the holy and profane.

3. R. L. Kotesky, *General Psychology for Christian Counselors* (Nashville: Abingdon Press, 1983), 165.

4. Bill O'Hanlon and James Wilk, *Shifting Contexts: The generation of effective psychotherapy* (New York: Guilford, 1987), 18.

5. G. A. Kelly, *A Theory of Personality: The psychology of personal constructs* (New York: Norton, 1965), 8–12.

6. Kotesky, *General Psychology*, 107.

7. David A. Carson, *God With Us: Themes from Matthew* (Ventura, Calif.: Regal Books, 1985), 77.

8. William Cormier and L. Sherilyn Cormier, *Interviewing Strategies for Helpers: Fundamental skills and cognitive behavioral interventions* (Pacific Grove, Calif.: Brooks/Cole, 1991), 217.

9. M. L. Bigge, *Learning Theories for Teachers* (New York: Harper & Row, 1976), 304.

10. Kotesky, *General Psychology*, 200–206.

11. L. Festinger, *A Theory of Cognitive Dissonance* (Evanston, Ill.: Row, Peterson, 1957).

12. Bigge, *Learning Theories*, 307.

13. Steve de Shazer, *Putting Difference to Work* (New York: Norton, 1991), 102.

Chapter Three

Reality Making

THE SPEAKER APPROACHED THE LECTERN to deliver the keynote address. As she began to speak lights blinked and meters bounced on the amplifier, and the audio technician dialed the controls to accurately reproduce her voice. Probably no one in the room thought about how the vibrations of the speaker's voice activated electrical impulses in the microphone, which transmitted them first to the amplifier and then to the loudspeakers where her words were reproduced. Even fewer listeners recognized that the sound waves hit their sensitive eardrums and the attached auricular bones, encoding the vibrations into impulses to be interpreted by the human brain as words, sentences, and paragraphs.

Just as the microphone picks up sound waves and translates them into electrical impulses measured by electronic instruments, so sound waves become impulses in the listener's nervous system. We manipulate impulses, not words, in our nervous systems. The same is also true when the eye, stimulated by light waves, passes impulses along the optic nerve to the brain where they are interpreted as images. Each person's *sense* of reality is actually a set of impulses representing what has stimulated the five senses. We comprehend these neurological messages by organizing and relating them to each other, but the impulses do not equal what they represent—they are not of the same order.[1]

An awareness of this neurological fact is important in order to understand how we construct our sense of reality. This chapter develops an explanation of this phenomenon and its impact on human understanding, communication, and counseling. In developing this explanation we consider several conceptions for the meanings we place on the information that passes our sense gates.

CONSTRUCTS

Kelly explains that the human mind uses templets to help analyze its surroundings:

> Man looks at his world through transparent patterns or templets which he creates and then attempts to fit over the realities of which the world is composed. The fit is not always very good. Yet without such patterns the world appears to be such an undifferentiated homogeneity that man is unable to make any sense out of it.[2]

Kelly called these patterns, or templets, *constructs*: "They are ways of construing the world. They are what enables man, and lower animals too, to chart a course of behavior." According to Kelly, attributions do not constitute actuality, but are representations of real physical events. Therefore, we are not describing a system which contends that reality is a figment of human imagination. Physical events are real and verifiable; but because humankind has the ability to represent them mentally, we are more than just responders to those events.

Kelly also maintains that people are scientists who investigate physical events. "The scientist's ultimate aim is to predict and control."[3] The individual human being who falls into the classification of scientist does nothing less than attempt to predict and control what will happen. We do this by guessing the pattern behind a given set of events. After making a guess, we set about to investigate more examples of the event to see if the prediction based on our guess comes about. If it does, we are rewarded and encouraged to guess again; but if it does not, we may be severely punished and discouraged about guessing again. Yet, we cannot escape the process of attempting to control and predict the environment for our own survival.

CLASSIFICATIONS

In order to understand our world, we divide what we perceive into categories so that similar things can be considered together. However, the events we investigate cannot be classified as belonging solely to one particular science such as psychology, physiology, or theology. Probably most readers have had the experience of taking on a job they did not fully understand. The only way to proceed was to divide and conquer—to reduce the mass into manageable chunks for analysis, synthesis, planning, and action. Studies of psychology, physiology, or theology (among others) attempt to understand the mass of available information from one perspective. The danger in dividing physical events into categories is that once assigned to a category, a bit of information, one that might just as legitimately belong to other classifications, is isolated from the investigative eye of other disciplines.

In the late 1960s I witnessed the efforts of literature, art, and music teachers to put their disciplines together in a study of the humanities. We wanted not to divide but to blend our classifications so we could understand the contributions each made to the other, for these arts were once all part of each other. Therefore, it was only fitting that they be placed in natural and historical relationship to each other for our better understanding. Yet this kind of relating of disciplines is unusual because we need to reduce what we observe to the lowest practical terms so we can grasp and understand the large amounts of data.

Thought influences perception. A biblical example discussed earlier illustrates this axiom. The children of Israel had completely defeated Jericho and moved on to attempt the same at Ai (Joshua 8). Because of sin in the camp, God allowed the Israelites to lose the battle. After purging the sin and sinners from the camp, Joshua again turned his attention to defeating Ai. This time, however, he prepared a diversion to trick the enemy into leaving their city. Then a band of Israelites could defeat and destroy it while Joshua trounced the besieged army of Ai in the field. Why did the leaders of Ai fall into this trap? They thought they could defeat the Israelites as they had before. Their past experience led them to predict what would happen, and they followed that prediction, not knowing about the Israelite ambush until it was too late. We might say they were defeated by strategy, when what we mean is they were tricked into *thinking* one thing when the opposite was actually the case.

In *Out of a Silent Planet*, C. S. Lewis says, "You cannot see things till you know roughly what they are."[4] This editorial comment is made just as a character arrives on a strange planet after a long space trip. In this strange, new place he must learn to see things in different colors and shapes. The vegetation on the strange planet is whitish-pink instead of green, and the blue sky is populated with rose-colored clouds that trick the otherwise experienced eye into disbelief. Only after gaining experience with the different colors and shapes on this unique planet could Lewis's character see clearly.

Perhaps you have had an experience similar to one I had recently. The secretary from our faculty offices was walking across the campus on her lunch break; I was walking toward her, but did not recognize her until she spoke to me. Why? I would have easily recognized her in the office setting, but when she was out of that setting I lost part of the association that triggered recognition. She was categorized in my mind as part of the office, but not part of the outdoor campus scene. Categorizing people, things, and information can keep us from valuable information that may be in us but classified in such a way that we cannot transfer it from one context to another.

Perhaps categorization is what kept the two disciples who walked with Jesus on the road to Emmaus from recognizing Him. Geldenhuys comments on the disciples' experience in this way: "Because they had never expected this and did not realize that He had really risen, and also because Jesus' resurrection body was not so easily recognizable owing to its heavenly nature, the two disciples did not recognize Him."[5] When finally they arrived in the village and the disciples persuaded Jesus to stay with them, He took the lead in praying and breaking the bread. Perhaps they had been at the feeding of the five thousand and there was something characteristic about how He prayed and broke the bread that caused the two disciples to recognize and conclude that this Man was indeed Jesus.[6] Luke records their recognition as "their eyes were opened" (Luke 24:31).

Mary of Magdala also failed to recognize Jesus when He appeared to her near the garden tomb (John 20:14). She thought He was the gardener (20:15b), and after she had classified the man to whom she spoke as a gardener, Mary did not reclassify Him as Jesus until He spoke her name. Maybe there was something in the tone, an inflection or a softness that caused Mary to change how she classified the man, and then of course, she recognized Him.

Children see life more literally than adults. Milton Erickson comments on how closed-minded adults can be:

> I gave a lecture to a large medical group, and when it was over, one of the doctors said, "I enjoyed your lecture and I followed your blackboard drawings, your illustrations, and explanations. Now, there is one thing I can't understand. Why didn't you use the poker that was lying in the trough? Why do you carry around the cane that you use for a poker?"
>
> I said, "I carry around a cane because I limp. It is also handy as a poker."
>
> He said, "You don't limp."
>
> And he learned that a lot of other members of the audience had not noticed that I limped. They just thought that it was an affectation, that I carried my cane in my pocket and then used it as a poker.
>
> I have walked into many homes and a small child has said right away, "What's wrong with your leg?" Because they notice that. A child's mind is a rather open thing. *Adults*

tend to restrict themselves. Every magician will tell you, "Don't let children too near or they will see through the trick." *Adults have closed minds.* They think they are watching everything. They aren't watching. *They have got a routine way of looking.*[7] (Emphasis added.)

Adults restrict themselves because they perceive life in stereotypical ways by categorizing and classifying information for ease of understanding. In this case Erickson got them to classify the cane as a pointer (poker) rather than as an aid for his limp. After they saw the cane as a pointer they could hardly accept that Erickson even had a limp. Classifying information is a necessary part of understanding, but, as Erickson's story illustrates, it can keep the observer-learner from using the same information in other classifications.

SCHEMATA

Jean Piaget, a contemporary of Kelly, also derived a system to explain human cognition but approached it from a developmental perspective. Piaget held there are two basic human abilities: organization, the "tendency to systematize and combine processes into coherent systems," and adaptation, "the tendency to adjust to the environment."[8] In order to provide stability in life, children and adults seek to balance their world views by self-regulation, a process Piaget called equilibration. Piaget labeled the patterns resulting from the process of organization and adaptation *schema*.

Schema (or schemata for the plural) change by two different mechanisms: assimilation and accommodation. Assimilation describes how parts of the environment are included in the schema. Accommodation accounts for the changes that must take place in the schema when elements of the environment are different enough not to be readily accepted in the existing schemata.

To illustrate what Piaget taught, consider how the appropriate sense detector picks up incoming sensory data and transmits them to the brain for collection and an attempt at understanding their meaning. If the sensory information matches or closely matches an existing pattern (schema), then we require no further recognition and classification. However, if the sensory information does not match any of the existing patterns (schemata), then the schema coming closest to matching it is modified to accommodate the new information. If the perceived information is too different, it may pass by the person entirely.

Consider how difficult it must have been for the teachers of Israel to miss the Son of God when He presented Himself to them so plainly. Jesus called them "blind guides" (Matt. 15:14) though He obviously did not mean they were physically blind. We describe their blindness as being of the heart, a poetic description for a blindness of the mind. They had their minds made up, we would say colloquially. Paul wrote of the same blindness in Eph. 1:18, "I pray also that the eyes of your heart may be enlightened." What is it about humankind that causes us to say their minds are darkened? First, there is spiritual darkness, an interpsychic condition resulting from the Fall; but second, the darkness can mean cognitive gloom, an intrapsychic condition resulting from not understanding the truth of God. Paul declares that emancipation from spiritual darkness begins with the delivery and reception of the Word of God which enlightens human understanding (Rom. 10:17).

ATTRIBUTION

O'Hanlon and Wilk distinguish between observable fact or evidence and the meanings or attributions people place on them.[9] Hundreds of bits of sensory information bombard us each minute. Most of this information we ignore or deselect in order to focus on data of primary interest. All sensory information would be an unintelligible mass if we did not attribute some meaning to it by comparing, contrasting, sorting, and categorizing input. The human brain adjusts itself to the data it receives. Irwin Moon of the Moody Institute of Science performed an experiment using himself as the subject. A pair of glasses was prepared so that when Moon wore them everything was turned upside down. After several days his brain adapted itself to the reversed sensory input and turned the image right side up. However, when the glasses were removed everything was upside down again and it took several days for Moon's brain to reverse the image. Moon's experiment illustrates the capability of the brain to organize and control sensory input.

Watzlawick explains philosophically as well as psychologically how we make personal realities out of the data coming through our sense gates.[10] He relates the results of the following experiment as an example of how we attribute our own meaning to physical events.

In one of many such experiments that the psychologist Alex Bavelas conducted at Stanford University many years ago (but unfortunately never published), the experimenter reads to the subject a long list of number pairs (e.g., 31 and 80, 77 and 15). After each pair the subject is supposed to say whether the two numbers "fit" or not. Invariably the subject first wants to know in what sense these numbers are supposed to "fit," and the experimenter explains that the task lies precisely in the discovery of these rules. This leads the subject to assume that his task is one of those usual trial-and-error experiments and that all he can therefore do is start out with random "fit" and "do not fit" responses. At first he is wrong every single time, but gradually his performance begins to improve and the "correct" responses of the experimenter increase. The subject thus arrives at a hypothesis that, although not entirely correct, turns out to be more and more reliable.

What the subject does not know is that there is no immediate connection between his guesses and the experimenter's reactions. The latter gives his "correct" responses on the basis of the ascending half of a bell-shaped curve, that is, very rarely at first, and then with increasing frequency. This creates in the subject an assumption of the order underlying the relation between the number pairs that can be so persistent that he is unwilling to relinquish it even after the experimenter has told him that his responses were noncontingent. Some subjects are even convinced of having discovered a regularity that the experimenter was unaware of.[11]

In this experiment, the subject found an attribution that "fits" but has no relationship to the plan of the experimenter. Well-meaning people who try to give an explanation for death or the birth of a deformed baby come close to this type of error. They take the events and attribute a meaning that cannot be verified. In an attempt to comfort, they even go so far as to guess what God is doing for the sufferer's benefit. The disciples of Jesus illustrated this concept when they debated the cause of a man's blindness (John 9). Did this man sin or did his parents, they wondered. Jesus was concerned over neither question, but let the disciples know that "this happened so that the work of God might be displayed in his (the blind man's) life." The disciples did not have enough categories or schemata to account for the reason this man was blind. They could only relate it to either the sin of this man or his parents. Jesus related it to the glory of God, an alternative schema.

Matthew records the reaction of Jesus' disciples on the night He came to them walking on the water. Their response reveals they had only one schema or attribution for whatever could walk on water. They knew it could not be a man; therefore, it could only be a ghost (Matt. 14:26), and so they concluded and were appropriately afraid.

Solomon (1 Kings 3:16–28) was confronted with an apparently unsolvable question. Two prostitutes were fighting over the custody of a single child. As the account unfolds, both women had given birth, but one had rolled over on her child during the night and killed him. The mother of the dead child switched babies and pretended the other mother's child had died and not her own. The dilemma was perpetuated by each claiming right to the child with no other person (or medical record) to witness which child belonged to which woman. The only apparent categories to answer the question were to give the child to either one woman or the other. Solomon in his wisdom added another category: give half to each woman. What he did was to destroy the attribution that the scheming mother had placed on the facts. This proposal revealed the true mother, and the problem was solved. When Israel learned of Solomon's wisdom, they recognized that it had come from God.

MAPPING

Bandler and Grinder, the founders of neuro-linguistic programming (NLP), a therapy model based on the work of Milton H. Erickson and other therapy systems, hold that human beings do not directly interact with the real world.[12] Rather, they develop cognitive maps of what they believe the real world to be and then behave according to that map. For example, when I want to go to a certain location in Chicago, I pull out a mental map (or perhaps a paper map) and plan my trip. Yet neither the mental map nor the paper map is the actual territory, for no traveler would put the paper map on the pavement in front of a car in an attempt to get where he wanted to go. We would think that insane; nevertheless, Bandler and Grinder maintain that we often mistake the map for the territory in our relationships with the world of people and things. Just as a paper map only represents the territory, so our cognitive maps only represent the real world. The more flaws there are in the map or the more the map is not filled in, the greater the errors we will make in relating to the real world.

Perhaps Paul wrote of how our understanding only maps the real world when he said, "Now we see but a poor reflection; then we shall see face to face. Now I know in part; then I shall know fully, even as I am fully known" (1 Cor. 13:12). F. W. Grosheide comments on this verse: "Our vision is not untrue, but it is imperfect as to its degree. When perfection has been reached *then* we shall see *face to face,* i.e., we shall with our eyes look straight in the face of things; there will be nothing between us and the things."[13] It seems, then, that we gain our knowledge of physical reality through a sifting process. We constantly gather bits of information about what is true, but only with cautious scientific effort. We hypothesize and test our guess for accuracy, while we maintain a willingness to be wrong should we discover more evidence.

Human perception is limited by neurological, social, and individual constraints.[14] I once told an adult Sunday school class that there was music, and even pictures, in the air around us. In spite of their incredulity I demonstrated what I meant by reminding them that radio and television waves were all around us, and we would only have to have a radio or television to hear and see what is invisible and silent to our eyes and ears. These electronic devices have their own special sensing mechanisms that allow them to pick up the pictures and sound in the air. We cannot hear and see these messages because we are not neurologically prepared to receive such data. We can only perceive what we are physically equipped to receive. Could there not be several dimensions of reality just outside our neurological ability to perceive?

In Genesis 11 God confused human language. By doing so He divided humankind into social groups, each speaking a common language and adhering to common social customs. An inability to understand each other resulted (Gen. 11:7), and the construction of the Tower of Babel stopped (Gen. 11:8). Now we are confronted with the same problem: We do not understand people of other language groups, and therefore we are separated from them. Although this constraint narrows our ability to communicate, it can be overcome by learning another language.

Misrepresentations

We all grow up in a world slightly different from other people, even our own siblings. Not everyone fears dogs, but when I was a young boy, I was severely bitten by a neighbor's dog. As a result, I developed a healthy respect for dogs, and even though today I have learned to get along with most dogs, I can feel that old fear rise up when a menacing dog startles me. This example can be multiplied endlessly in the lives of people who have individual, personal experiences with seemingly numberless life elements. Two people who experience the same event can develop different personal meanings for that same incident, and the millions of events combine and recombine to produce a unique understanding of the world in each person.[15]

What does this mean? Bandler and Grinder believe that problems arise from inaccuracies in our cognitive maps and that the way out of problems is to make the maps more accurate in their representation of the world. Language is a key to understanding how a client maps the real world, and understanding the formation of language is essential to learning how the map is incorrect or incomplete.[16]

People misread the real world in three different ways. The first is *generalization,* "the process by which a specific experience comes to represent the entire category of which it is a member."[17] Although it is a necessary learning tool to transfer knowledge from one context to another, generalization can also narrow the person's experience—if the learner takes, for example, a bad experience and transfers it to other similar situations. Prejudice, though based on a single experience or the views of others, keeps the person from appreciating the individual differences of people from various ethnic and racial backgrounds.

Consider how generalization misled the leaders of Ai when they set about to defeat Israel the second time. Their first victory over Israel was in their minds; if they could win once, they believed they could win again. Battle situation one was equated with battle situation two through generalization. Unfortunately for Ai the two battle situations were entirely different, even though that difference was unclear to them.

The second means of misreading reality is *deletion,* "a process by which we selectively pay attention to certain dimensions of our experience and exclude others."[18] Chapter 2 outlined how we deselect stimuli that bombard us so we can operate on a manageable amount of information. What we leave out of our awareness Bandler and Grinder label as deletions. Deleting is necessary in learning, but it can leave the person with an unclear representation of physical reality. Consider a counselee who has come to believe, based on some experiences, that he or she is not accepted in social situations. Once this generalization is established, the counselee must then delete from awareness all situations where acceptance is provided. The limited world view impoverishes the counselee in such a way that choices are eliminated.

For example, "My husband never helps me around the house," cries a distraught wife. This generalization leads to a deletion in her map of physical reality. Reality would probably reveal that her husband does help her with some activities around the house, but these behaviors have been excluded from her thinking. She had deleted them from her map of reality.

Consider also how God purposely changed Peter's mind about clean and unclean things by teaching him a lesson in the rooftop trance (Acts 10:9–23). Peter followed the current religious teachings by keeping himself from eating anything unclean. Unclean animals had been deleted from his diet. However, God wanted Peter to recognize that not all things declared unclean by the religious establishment are unclean. This included Peter's relationship with the Gentiles. The generalization that uncleanness encompassed the Gentiles meant that Peter would not have considered sharing the gospel with them if God had not intervened and removed the generalization.

Peter also illustrates the last way that we misread our physical reality. "*Distortion* is the process which allows us to make shifts in our experience of sensory data."[19] As I write this chapter I must distort my present experience to imagine how you, as the reader, may understand what I have written. My preferred way of distortion in this case is to hear what I have written as though I were speaking to you. In order to do that I must shut out other sounds in the room. Noise around me keeps me from focusing on you. Peter's trance provides a classic biblical example of distortion (Acts 10:9–23). His visual and auditory perception had to be focused on the distorted perception of the sheet, animals, and voice of God. Other perceptual experiences at the time were excluded.

So people are hindered because they generalize, delete, and distort their perceptions of physical reality. They are also limited neurologically, socially, and individually from fully grasping the world around them. All of these limitations give each person a unique understanding of the world. No two people, no matter how much time they have together, would share the very same view of physical reality, and the degree to which they misrepresent physical reality is also the degree to which they are hampered in solving life problems.

SIGNIFICANCE

Why is the fact that human beings operate on maps, schemata, constructs, classifications or attributions so important? Just this: a troubled person approaches a counselor to solve a problem that has not yielded to any solutions. It is the counselor's responsibility to help the counselee find a different map—one more useful in solving the problem. It is also the counselor's responsibility to help the client realign the elements of the problem so it can be solved.

A man in his late twenties came to my office and told me how anxious he was feeling. After a few questions he revealed that he was getting a divorce from his wife of eight years and that he was also starting a new relationship with another woman who seemed eager to become intimate sooner than my client was prepared for. He needed more time to get over his feelings of loss. He was caught between those feelings and the urging of his girlfriend.

As part of the interview I learned that his family had moved several times as he was growing up. I asked how he had coped with loss each time his family had moved. After thinking a few minutes, he told me his dog moved with him each time, and the dog was a real comfort to him. Then I was able to tell him that he was an expert in loss, and that he knew how to experience grief given the proper amount of time. His new girlfriend would have to give him the time to handle his own experience of personal loss.[20] He visibly relaxed and said he would speak to his girlfriend about giving him time to recover.

Two weeks later he reported that she had agreed with his request and the development of their relationship was less intense. He said he felt much calmer and did not need another appointment. Getting over a loss is easier to understand and accept than having anxiety. What he needed was time, and with the new way of defining his problem he was able to ask for what he needed. Once he viewed his problem as a kind of loss, a subject in which he was an expert, he was able to solve the problem himself.

The fact that people place meanings on the data they receive through the sense gates allows the counselor to help them find more acceptable and useful ways of understanding what is happening to them. The next chapter provides a summary of solutions which will be referred to in succeeding chapters. It also provides a general inquiry into what changes when counseling is successful.

NOTES

1. Jay Efran, M. Lukens, and R. Lukens, *Language, Structure, and Change: Frameworks of meaning in psychotherapy* (New York: Norton, 1990), 67–68.

2. G. A. Kelly, *A Theory of Personality: The psychology of personal constructs* (New York: Norton, 1963), 9.

3. Kelly, *A Theory of Personality*, 5.

4. C. S. Lewis, *Out of a Silent Planet* (New York: Macmillan, 1965), 42.

5. N. Geldenhuys, *Commentary on the Gospel of Luke* (Grand Rapids, Mich.: Eerdmans, 1951), 632.

6. Geldenhuys, *Commentary on the Gospel of Luke*, 635.

7. Sidney Rosen, ed., *My Voice Will Go with You: The teaching tales of Milton H. Erickson, M.D.* (New York: Norton, 1982), 180–181.

8. R. Biehler, *Child Development: An introduction* (Boston: Houghton Mifflin, 1976), 154.

9. Bill O'Hanlon and James Wilk, *Shifting Contexts: The generation of effective psychotherapy* (New York: Guilford, 1987).

10. Paul Watzlawick, *Munchhausen's Pigtail: or Psychotherapy & "reality" essays and lectures* (New York: Norton, 1990), 85–88

11. Paul Watzlawick, *The Invented Reality* (New York: Norton, 1984), 13–14

12. Richard Bandler and John Grinder, *The Structure of Magic,* 2 vols. (Palo Alto, Calif.: Science and Behavior Books, 1975).

13. F. W. Grosheide, *Commentary on the First Epistle to the Corinthians* (Grand Rapids, Mich.: Eerdmans, 1953), 311.

14. Bandler and Grinder, *Structure of Magic*, vol. 1, 8–13.

15. Moshe Talmon, *Single-Session Therapy: Maximizing the effect of the first (and often only) therapeutic encounter* (San Francisco: Jossey-Bass, 1990), 123.

16. Efran, Lukens, and Lukens, *Language, Structure, and Change*, 146–148.

17. Bandler and Grinder, *Structure of Magic*, vol. 1, 216.

18. Ibid. p. 15.

19. Ibid. p. 16.

20. Steve de Shazer, *Putting Difference to Work* (New York: Norton, 1991), 82.

Chapter Four

Basics of Successful Counseling

W HAT CHANGES WHEN COUNSELING IS SUCCESSFUL? Counselors who understand how people think about themselves and their problems are better able to assist counselees in handling whatever situation led them to seek help. Many theories of psychotherapy, secular and Christian, strive to change how people think: Albert Ellis's rational emotive therapy, Larry Crabb's biblical counseling, William Glasser's reality therapy, Jay Adam's nouthetic counseling, and what is generally known as behavioral therapy. Each of these will be considered briefly, followed by summaries of Steve de Shazer's solution focused therapy, Alfred Adler's individual psychology, Albert Bandura's efficacy expectancy, and the adaptive counseling and therapy metamodel.

RATIONAL EMOTIVE THERAPY

Rational emotive therapy (RET) grew out of the practice of Albert Ellis, a native New Yorker, who believes that people are in trouble because they are thinking incorrectly about themselves, others, and the world. RET is called the "ABCD" model of counseling: "A" is the activating event—the activity, action, or agent that disturbs the individual. The "C" is the consequent behavior and/or feeling. Most people identify "A" as the cause of the feeling or behavior. But Ellis points out that "A" does not cause the problem, but rather "B," the belief about "A." This belief results in the painful consequence "C" that ultimately brings the person to the counselor. It is useless to attack the "A" (activating event) that is in the past or out of the control of the counselee and counselor. However, it is practical to identify and dispute ("D") the disturbing beliefs ("B") about "A."

BIBLICAL COUNSELING

Biblical counseling, framed by Larry Crabb, starts very much like RET but goes further and attempts to discover the misbeliefs that substitute for the way God wants us to believe. People attempt to get their needs for significance and security met by ill-advised and useless schemes emanating from non-Christian, self-centered, and/or evil beliefs. The biblical counselor identifies the wrong behavior and the underlying feelings. Once these are known, therapy centers on the beliefs that support the feelings and behaviors. These beliefs are necessarily ungodly and useless, and the person is advised to abandon them and adopt biblical beliefs that can then lead to right feelings and godly behavior, resulting in true success and joy.

REALITY THERAPY

The reality therapist also recognizes the counselee's need for significance and security, but focuses on irresponsible behavior rather than misguided beliefs. William Glasser developed reality therapy (RT) at a school for girls and at a veterans' hospital. Glasser departed from his psychoanalytic training to concentrate on what his patients were doing that was so unsuccessful. By holding the patients responsible for reasonable and normal behavior, Glasser achieved remarkable results in a relatively short time.

RT has evolved since the mid-1960s so that now the reality therapist uses a step approach to solving problems very similar to the four-step model presented in this book. These steps include developing a relationship with the counselee, identifying the unproductive or harmful behavior, setting appropriate goals, and getting the person to commit to a responsible daily change that will lead to improved feelings and thoughts. The reality therapist holds the person accountable, but does not criticize his or her failure to keep a commitment. Each counseling appointment starts at the beginning step and ends with a commitment to a behavior that will lead to a mature and successful life pattern.

NOUTHETIC COUNSELING

Jay Adams (nouthetic counseling) also holds the individual responsible for his or her behavior, but from a biblical perspective. Troubled people must bring their behavior into conformity with the teachings of the Bible before they can expect happiness and success. Whereas Glasser (RT) resorts to social convention for his guidelines, Adams uses the infallible Word to teach his counselees how to normalize their lives. For example, a man may have difficulties with headaches, fatigue, and stomach problems. The nouthetic counselor would look for the ways the man is violating the Word of God, and then teach the biblical principles and precepts that must become a part of his life before he can expect to recover. If the counselee is not a Christian, the first consideration is commitment to Christ and then to biblical behaviors that yield a healthier and happier life.

BEHAVIOR THERAPY

Behavior therapy also focuses on changing behavior; it is based on a learning theory that developed from nearly one hundred years of research. Because they cannot know for certain what happens inside a person, behavior theorists do not attempt to change beliefs or attitudes. They focus instead on the troubling behavior itself. These changes are accomplished through various behavioral techniques, one of which is desensitization. Desensitization begins by putting a counselee's fears into a hierarchical order from the least fearful to the most fearful. The therapist also teaches the counselee how to relax voluntarily. When this is accomplished, the therapist presents, in imagery, the least fearful object or event and helps the counselee relax while thinking about the feared object. Once success is obtained at one level, they proceed to more fearful objects (and emotional events) until all are conquered and the counselee is able to take what was learned in therapy into daily life. The behavior therapist treats the counselee's value system with respect, and does not attempt to place his or her values on the counselee as we see in many Christian theories.

Efficacy Expectancy

When considering the question, "What changes when an individual gets better?" we need to consider the work of Albert Bandura, a learning theorist who made significant contributions to modern education. Our consideration of Bandura's work examines his research with phobic people. Bandura worked with clients who were afraid of snakes, reasoning that they were least likely to decrease their fear by learning experiences outside of the experimental laboratory.

Two initial concepts are integral to the understanding of Bandura's work: outcome expectancy and efficacy expectancy. Outcome expectancy is the expectation that a given behavior will lead to certain outcomes. Efficacy expectation, as defined by Bandura, seems to be confidence one has in the ability to behave in ways that will produce the outcomes.[1] Those people with low efficacy expectancy, or low confidence, could have high outcome expectancy but not believe they are able to perform adequately the necessary actions. These are people who think, "I could never do this (low efficacy expectancy), but if I could change my behavior I know I would do better (high outcome expectancy)." Such a belief would keep them from trying.

A lowered efficacy expectancy is characteristic of individuals who have had an accident. Common-sense suggestions to "get back on the horse," "remember, you can do it," or "get going again," reflect a desire to restore efficacy expectancy. People with a lower efficacy expectancy may suffer from severe discouragement and depression. Helping counselees understand what is discouraging them and what they can do to overcome these obstacles often helps them utilize their resources more effectively, thus relieving the depression.

Efficacy expectancy is better understood when it is crossed with outcome expectancy as illustrated in figure 4–1.

	No, it won't work	Yes, it will work
Yes, I can do it	Person believes the situation will not change but not because he or she is incapable. Therefore person does not berate himself or herself.	Person believes the situation can change and he or she has the ability to bring about a successful outcome.
No, I can't do it	Person does not believe he or she can change. Person believes that the situation will not readily change anyway.	Person believes situation could change but has no confidence in his or her ability to do what is necessary to bring reform.

Efficacy Expectancy *(left axis label)*

Outcome Expectancy *(bottom axis label)*

Efficacy Grid[2]
Figure 4–1

People usually want to succeed but may be lacking in either efficacy expectancy (confidence) or outcome expectancy, possibly both. Often they need to learn what lies within the realm of possibility. Others may know the possibilities, but do not believe they have the skills or self-confidence to accomplish their goal. Developing skills is an important part of counseling.

Using phobic people, Bandura researched the best way to alter the level and strength of efficacy expectancy. He maintained that personal efficacy expectations stem from four main sources: (1) performance accomplishments based on past experience (the strongest source of information); (2) vicarious experiences, watching another person try and then succeed; (3) verbal persuasion, convincing someone by argument that he or she can perform successfully; and (4) emotional arousal, emotional distress signaling that something is wrong and that the individual cannot accomplish the task as laid out.[3] "Perceived self-efficacy is concerned with people's judgments of how well they can organize and execute constituent cognitive, social, and behavioral skills in dealing with prospective situations."[4]

People avoid activities they believe exceed their coping capabilities, but they undertake and perform assuredly those that they judge themselves capable of managing.[5] Stage fright illustrates how emotional distress may erode confidence. The normal emotional arousal that occurs when someone speaks in public tends to reduce that person's ability to think and remember. This causes more anxiety, creating a downward spiral that ultimately leads to an avoidance of all public speaking. Teaching a person with stage fright how to control the emotional response, and then actually going through a frightening experience, exemplifies experiential modeling, the most effective means of improving confidence. Persistence, then, pays off in lessons that tell the individual how to correct future behavior and thus assure future success; whereas quitting only decreases confidence because the person has no feedback about how to change behavior to make it successful.[6] Fear arises when an individual does not believe that he or she is capable of handling a situation.

Confidence, or efficacy expectation, and outcome expectancy do not replace motivation. People can have both confidence and outcome expectancy and still not perform if they do not want to, if they see no benefit to themselves, or if the task seems too easy. They need a moderate challenge to encourage them. If a task is too easy or too hard, it is unlikely they will try. Confidence determines how hard and for how long an individual will attempt a task. Therefore, it is important to estimate accurately the level of confidence counselees have before assigning a task. Obviously, those with less confidence need to perform easier tasks until they have built their confidence level through successful experiences. Once people decide they are incapable (low confidence), they dwell on their inabilities rather than on how to cope with the undesired situation. They "awfulize"[7] and magnify their concerns, further limiting their range of responses. This assures continued failure.[8]

Bandura's work provides counselors with a theoretical background for intervention into the lives of counselees. A theoretical foundation such as this permits counselors to generalize over various kinds of individuals, problems, and situations.

SOLUTION FOCUSED THERAPY

Because confidence has such a strong influence on how much and how long a person struggles with a problem, the counselor must consider confidence in the process of evaluating clients. Changing confidence becomes a focus of therapy in many, if not all cases. By getting clients to believe in the ability of the counselor, most counseling systems, whether they admit it or not, seek to influence people's confidence.

Few systems, however, make building confidence the single target of therapy. In contrast, Steve de Shazer and his associates developed solution focused therapy, a unique approach to short-term counseling that clearly attempts to persuade counselees that they are able to solve their problems.[9]

Solution focused therapy intervenes from the very beginning of counseling. Like efficacy expectancy in Bandura's theory, solution focused therapy recognizes from the start that people who are discouraged and low in confidence are kept from solving the problem. The solution focused therapist also believes that most people have the ability to solve their problems but have become convinced that they are not able to do so. To convince them that they are capable, the solution focused therapist must change how counselees think about their ability to make a difference in the problem situation. This is accomplished by several interventions beginning in the first few minutes of the counseling session.

The first intervention gets the clients talking about what has changed in their lives since they contacted the counselor. Solution focused counselors ask their counselees whether the problem has altered in any way since they made the initial appointment.[10] Informal research reveals that about two thirds of people asked acknowledge some change. The solution focused counselor attempts to build the change into a solution for the problem by asking how the change came about, who was involved, who made the difference, and other factual questions. Together they build the answers into a comprehensive solution for the problem.

Problems rarely happen consistently, and asking for the exceptions—the second type of intervention—uncovers those times when the problem is not there. Focusing on the exceptions starts people thinking about solutions instead of problems. When there are exceptions, ask "What is different about the times when the problem does not happen?" Here, again, look for who, what, where, and other factual questions designed to reveal differences between when the problem is and is not occurring.

A third solution focused intervention asks individuals to imagine that a miracle has occurred and the problem is now solved. "What is different?" "Who noticed first?" "What did each person do differently?" are some of the questions de Shazer asks to stimulate solution focused problem solving. The miracle question puts the solution into focus and allows people to see the problem in light of the solution. The solution then becomes conceivable and possible.

The de Shazer group has counseled hundreds of individuals and couples and has done research into the effectiveness of their approach. They typically end treatment by the fifth session.[11] Contact made six months to one year later indicates that counselees have not sought other assistance and consider the problem solved.[12] This unusual counseling system and its results raises the question of how they accomplish such changes. What is unique about the solution focused approach?

Solution focused therapy influences the counselee's confidence level. Bandura defined efficacy expectation in such a way that he seemed to mean confidence. People who come to solution focused counselors are just as discouraged as the persons choosing other forms of therapy. The difference is that solution focused counselors seek to change the counselee's confidence level as quickly as possible. Elevating confidence has a profound influence on the problem because people who believe they can make a difference try harder and longer to solve the problem.

ADLERIAN COUNSELING

What makes Adlerian counseling effective? The Adlerian counselor uses encouragement to change the counselee's approach to problems. Troubled people are discouraged, and they need encouragement that will change their confidence level and stimulate them to make the effort devoted to solving the problem. Changing people's confidence levels is a simple but elegant intervention.

Raymond Corsini relates an experience with a prisoner who made an abrupt and extraordinary change as a result of a simple statement made by Corsini.[13] Just before his parole, the prisoner asked for an appointment where he thanked Corsini for his help two years earlier. Corsini could not remember seeing the man and wondered just what had made such an effective change. The prisoner reported that Corsini had said, "You told me I have a high IQ." Just that short sentence had changed that man's life in a dramatic way. When he left Corsini that day he felt like an entirely new person.

Early in life, the prisoner had learned from experience that other people thought him stupid and crazy. He had earned poor grades in school, and his friends labeled him as strange because they did not agree with him. He gradually accepted these judgments about himself and drifted into crime. He was discouraged, yet changed almost miraculously when Corsini interpreted his IQ score as being above average. The way he viewed himself changed in that session, as did his confidence level. The prisoner reported, "When I left your office . . . , I felt like I was walking on air. When I went into the prison yard everything looked different, even the air smelled different."[14] Changing people by altering their confidence level works and makes good sense for all those who help people, especially for counselors who are limited by how much time they can devote to each person.

ADAPTIVE COUNSELING AND THERAPY METAMODEL

Adaptive counseling and therapy (ACT) is a metamodel, a model of models, which, on the basis of three discernible personal qualities, selects the style of counseling that would best fit the counselee.[15] The level or presence of competence, confidence, and motivation allows helpers to place people into one of four categories, as illustrated in figure 4–2, which has been adapted from the adaptive counseling and therapy metamodel.[16] Those who lack competence, confidence, and motivation fall into the first quadrant, Q1, where they would receive maximum direction but little support. When people have some motivation but lack competence and

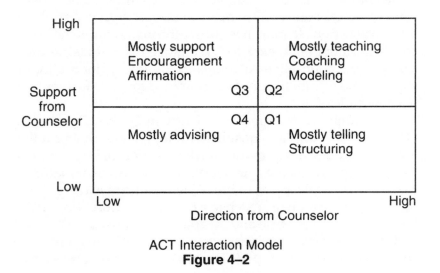

ACT Interaction Model
Figure 4–2

confidence, they require both support and direction, as seen in Q2. Mostly support and little direction (Q3) is appropriate for counselees who have some measure of competence, confidence, and motivation. Those who have considerable levels of all three fit best into Q4, where they need little direction or support.

To illustrate, use the ACT model to evaluate a person named John. Deficits in competence, confidence, and motivation place John in quadrant 1 (Q1) indicating a need to have the relationship with the counselor structured by strictly observed rules, including specific starting and ending times for counseling. If available, testing would introduce more structure and could also help determine John's style of dealing with life issues. People like John often enter counseling because someone else demands that they get help—often the court, a wife, or parents—and John probably does not see the need for it. Converting him into a motivated counselee is one of the counselor's first goals.

If John were motivated but lacked competence and confidence, he would fall into Q2, where he would receive large amounts of teaching and coaching. The counselor must model new behavior and then cheer him on as John practices different living patterns. When John is motivated and has built up some competence but is still lacking in confidence, he moves from Q2 to Q3 and receives mostly support with very little, if any, instruction. If John has difficulty managing in Q3, the counselor moves him back to Q2, a move that avoids extreme shifts in the counseling relationship. By giving John a lot of support and affirmation, he is encouraged to move further into his new style of life.

When John has matured sufficiently in Q3, he advances to Q4. Here the counselor consults with John about different life issues, but does not provide much direction or support. Q4 therapy depends on the counselee's having sufficient maturity to handle the basic issues of life. When maturity wavers, there may be a temptation to switch to a Q1 style of counseling. This, however, would confuse and infuriate the counselee. The general rule is to move back just one quadrant at a time until the counselee is stabilized. (Shifting back and forth between Q1 and Q4 describes what parents often do to their children, and is a style that can perplex the most mature child.)

The attractiveness of the ACT metamodel is its flexibility over various counseling approaches and widely different counseling problems and counselee styles. It serves as a guide to making decisions about the style of treatment that would likely be successful. The counselor makes an assessment of the client by determining the level of motivation, competence, and confidence. Based on this assessment, the counselor estimates the needs of the client and the style that should work best for that particular person. When the style is not known, or in the first few minutes of the counseling process and until an assessment is made, it is best to use a Q3 style.

ENCOURAGEMENT THERAPY

All of the above systems of counseling aim at changing people either by changing beliefs or by changing behavior. Counseling can make a difference, but just *what* changes is still not clear. To answer this question consider the person's frame of mind when he or she asks for counseling.

People who seek help are often, if not always, discouraged and convinced that there is little or nothing they can do to make the problem any better. Adlerian counselors refuse to identify their counselees with pathological labels, preferring to classify troubled people as discouraged. Discouragement begins early in life and surfaces in adulthood when individuals face difficulties beyond their knowledge and experience or, at least, what they think is beyond them. It does not matter whether or not they are capable, for when people think they cannot, they will not even try. This is the attitude that the pastoral counselor often encounters when asked for help.

DISCOURAGEMENT

Discouraged and disenhearted are apt adjectives for how people are thinking when they come for help. What changes in counseling, then, is the attitude, disposition, or opinion of the counselee. Reconsider the prisoner with the above-average IQ discussed in the earlier example. He made an abrupt and extraordinary change as a result of a simple statement made by Corsini. However, as a result of Corsini's brief intervention in his life, the prisoner completely changed his associates, took a job where he could learn a trade, finished high school, and had a job waiting for him when he was paroled. The story illustrates a remarkable change as the result of a seemingly trivial intervention. What changed?

Apparently the prisoner had concluded that he was a defective person who had little hope of success in life. He acted out his belief about himself when he turned to crime. This story illustrates what Alfred Adler would term discouragement, a condition afflicting those who are not successful in life. Although a contemporary of Sigmund Freud, Adler developed a theory of pathology very different from Freud's psychoanalysis. Freud's theory depicts people as driven by instinctual drives, but Adler saw people as drawn by some purpose meaningful to them even though the resultant behavior is harmful and/or antisocial. The prisoner's criminal behavior met his need to be significant and was consistent with the belief about himself describing him as abnormal and unable to compete with others in a successful way.

Some telltale signs of discouragement are:

Excessive need for attention
Need for power and control
Need for revenge
Dishonesty
Need for perfection
Closed-mindedness
Avoidance of competition
Avoidance of responsibility
Lack of confidence
Thoughts of worthlessness[17]

Add to these signs the hatred and murder characterizing the thinking and motivation behind some biblical characters. Cain was discouraged about his relationship with God when he started hating Abel. King Saul wanted to destroy David because he knew the people of Israel considered David a greater warrior and more popular hero. Judas betrayed Jesus out of a desire for superiority that resulted from a deep sense of inferiority. Discouragement is not a sin in itself, but it certainly may lead to sinful acts.

Discouragement describes the thinking of people who come for counsel. They have tried to solve their problems and have not found a workable solution. Friends and other concerned helpers have contributed their solutions, but these have not worked either. They have nowhere to turn. This makes their request for help desperate and crucial.

ENCOURAGEMENT

In spite of their discouragement, people must have some measure of faith in counseling or they would not seek treatment. Developing this small faith into significant change is the first, and possibly only, task of successful counseling. Losoncy, an Adlerian counselor, emphasizes the importance of encouragement—especially unconditional positive regard and acceptance, both crucial attitudes for the counselor to hold toward clients.[18] The counselor must suspend judgment, letting people express what is hidden from others but is so harmful to themselves. Deeply sensing another's pain eases burdens. Helpers must believe that those they attempt to help would be able, if they were not discouraged, to solve their problems. People usually consider only accomplishments and discount or ignore attempts, but encouragers are enthusiastic about effort. The fact that you are reading this book is commendable because you are making an effort to become a better counselor. Pat yourself on the back; encourage yourself and note how good it feels. This is the same feeling that helps start troubled people on the way to successful life changes.

Are you an encouragement to others, like Barnabas in the Book of Acts? Are you able to turn a weakness into a strength? Do people come to you because you send them away lifted and ready to meet life's challenges? Do you encourage yourself? Is your theology encouraging? Do you see God as an encourager?

Troubled people are discouraged, not crazy. They want encouragement from life and come to the counselor for that encouragement. As illustrated in the earlier story about the prisoner, encouragement can have startling results.

Counselors can learn to encourage others effectively by cultivating a positive attitude and meaningful communication techniques.

Psychology and common sense confirm the importance of encouragement, but what does the Bible have to say about encouragement? The Lord encourages the afflicted when He listens to their cry (Isa. 1:17). God commanded Isaiah to encourage the oppressed; and He ranks encouragement with seeking justice, defending the fatherless, and pleading the cases of widows. Encouragement is a spiritual gift to be used freely (Rom. 12:8). Paul identifies Scripture as a source of encouragement and God as the giver of both endurance and encouragement (Rom. 15:4–5). In 1 Thess. 4:18 and 5:11, Paul commands Christians to encourage each other and, in Titus 1:9, to use sound doctrine. The writer to the Hebrews says, "But encourage one another daily, as long as it is called Today, so that none of you may be hardened by sin's deceitfulness" (Heb. 3:13). Here encouragement is associated with protecting the believer from callousness—every believer is responsible to encourage others daily. The importance of Christian encouragement is clearly documented biblically, and the sources of encouragement are identified as God, Scripture, sound doctrine, and people.

Encouraging others demands qualities rarely found in people. First, encouraging requires courage in the helper because lifting another demands reaching out to the sensitive and tender person hiding behind protective emotional barriers.[19] Most of us lean away from people rather than toward them, and we rationalize our distancing as not wanting to intrude in the personal lives, beliefs, and desires of others. We are actually protecting ourselves from the tenderness which makes all of us feel exposed and uncomfortable.

Second, encouragers are readily gracious, accepting, and slow to criticize and blame. But many Christian helpers, quick to judge and slow to encourage, forget the spiritual significance of encouragement and become self-appointed critics. Graciousness and acceptance permeate encouragement and soften criticism, helping the other person benefit from the human interaction.[20]

Genuineness, a third personal quality, does not mean the helper is perfect, but aware of his or her personal problems and willing to face them honestly. A genuine person is not just playing a role; he or she is truly concerned about other people. If we act as though we are concerned when in fact we are not, the other person senses this contradiction, invalidates our efforts, and distrusts our motives.

Finally, Crabb and Allender stress the importance commitment has on encouraging.[21] Because encouraging requires that we reach beyond ourselves, we must also not worry about our own needs being met at that time. Encouraging another person is not always comfortable, but commitment takes us beyond our feelings to do what is best for another person.

By now it is probably obvious that encouraging is more than just a pat on the back and a "Cheer up, friend." I have chosen to call this deep, concerted effort to help other people think and feel differently about themselves Encouragement Therapy.

FINALLY

The thrust of this chapter has been to answer the question, "What changes when counseling is successful?" We have looked for the answer from several theoretical positions. Adlerians believe troubled people are discouraged and lack the confidence to accomplish life tasks. Confidence or efficacy expectancy is central in the theory of change researched by Albert Bandura, who also helped us to understand that the best way of helping phobic people is to model or demonstrate new behavior and then support them as they face the fearful object. We also noted from Bandura's research that verbal persuasion is a less effective way of changing people, and from de Shazer's that solution focused counselors kindle change by focusing on exceptions. Some, if not all, of solution focused success is based on finding factual evidence from the counselee's life that demonstrates competence, thus elevating the confidence level. Elevating confidence significantly affects performance, and raising confidence levels is an initial, if not, major component of successful counseling.

The adaptive counseling and therapy (ACT) metamodel uses confidence level as one determining factor in choosing the style of counseling most likely to be successful. By taking the central component from these several theories, encouragement therapy attempts to answer the question put before us in this chapter: What changes when counseling is successful?

NOTES

1. Albert Bandura, Nancy Adams, and Janice Beyer, "Cognitive processes mediating behavioral changes," *Journal of Personality and Social Psychology* 35, no. 3 (March 1977): 126.

2. Albert Bandura, "Self-efficacy mechanisms in human agency," *American Psychologist* 37, no. 2 (1982):140. Figure 4–1 adapts and expands Bandura's conceptualization.

3. Bandura, Adams, and Beyer, "Cognitive processes," 126.

4. Albert Bandura, "Self-efficacy determinants of anticipated fears and calamities," *Journal of Personality and Social Psychology* 45, no. 2 (1983):467.

5. See Albert Bandura, "Self-efficacy mechanisms," 123; and Moshe Talmon, *Single-Session Therapy: Maximizing the effect of the first (and often only) therapeutic encounter* (San Francisco: Jossey-Bass, 1990), 120.

6. Bandura, Adams, and Beyer, "Cognitive processes," 126.

7. Albert Ellis coined "awfulize" to describe the human tendency to make things worse than they really are.

8. Bandura, "Self-efficacy mechanisms," 137.

9. Steve de Shazer, *Putting Difference to Work* (New York: Norton, 1991), 56–59.

10. Steve de Shazer and Barbara Backlund, *The Twenty Minute Counselor: Transforming brief conversations into effective helping experiences* (New York: Continuum, 1991), 53–59.

11. Steve de Shazer, *Keys to Solutions in Brief Therapy* (New York: Norton, 1985), *xvii*.

12. Steve de Shazer et al., "Brief therapy: Focused solution development," *Family Process* 25 (1986):219.

13. Richard Corsini and Danny Wedding, *Current Psychotherapies* (Itasca, Ill.: F. E. Peacock, 1989), 4.

14. Corsini and Wedding, *Current Psychotherapies*, 3.

15. G. Howard, D. Nance, and P. Myers, *Adaptive Counseling and Therapy: A systematic approach to selecting effective treatments* (San Francisco: Jossey-Bass, 1987).

16. Howard, Nance, and Myers, *Adaptive Counseling and Therapy*, 45.

17. L. Losoncy, *Turning People On: How to be an encouraging person* (Englewood Cliffs, N.J.: Prentice-Hall, 1977), 10.

18. Losoncy, *Turning People On*, 88.

19. Larry Crabb and D. Allender, *Encouragement: The key to caring* (Grand Rapids, Mich.: Zondervan, 1984), 48.

20. Gerard Egan, *The Skilled Helper: A systematic approach to effective helping,* 4th ed. (Pacific Grove, Calif.: Brooks/Cole, 1990), 389–391.

21. Crabb and Allender, *Encouragement,* 47–54.

Chapter Five

Social Stage

MILTON H. ERICKSON WRITES of a paranoid patient who walked around the hospital wrapped in a bed sheet and claimed to be Jesus Christ. Erickson and the patient took a walk around the grounds of the hospital one day. They talked about the trees that God had made, the beauty of the grass, and of God's creation in general.

They passed the tennis courts used by the doctors to keep themselves in good physical condition. As they did Erickson pointed out that the dirt court contained several rough spots. He explained to the patient that he was sure God didn't want those rough spots on the court and asked if the patient could see to it that the courts were leveled and nicely groomed. The patient indicated that he was there to serve mankind and would do his best to take care of it. Erickson left him at that point, and the man became an excellent groundskeeper for the tennis courts.

When the psychology laboratory needed some bookcases built, Erickson asked this paranoid young man for assistance with some carpentry work. How could the patient refuse and maintain his illness? The bookshelves were built and the young man was employed with other tasks around the hospital.[1]

Although some might argue that the patient was being used (to keep the grounds and build bookshelves), this case illustrates how Erickson accepted the counselee's world view and used it to help the patient live more productively. Actually, the patient had only two choices: accept the assignment and keep his psychotic identity or reject the assignment and his belief that he was Jesus Christ.

Erickson developed rapport with his patient. What is rapport?[2] Fischer defines rapport as a relationship of mutual respect.[3] He maintains that personal relationships develop because each person contributes significant elements to start and maintain the relationship. In the counseling relationship these relational elements include: (1) the counselor's recognition that the therapeutic alliance is too complicated to assert that only a few variables contribute to its maintenance; (2) the counselor's recognition that the counselee is not mechanistically controlled, but a dynamic contributor in the relationship; (3) the counselor's recognition that the counselee is not an object to be manipulated; and (4) the counselor's recognition and maintenance of the counselee's integrity as essential to sustaining the rapport.

The therapeutic work of Erickson embodies the guidelines outlined by Fischer. The counselee behaves ". . . in terms of what the situation means to him."[4] Rapport is an interactive social process. Ideally, developing rapport in counseling begins with the counselor and counselee understanding each other's perspectives, as in the case of the patient who thought he was Jesus Christ.

Another of Erickson's cases involved a medical student who had withdrawn from normal social relationships after he had lost his leg in an accident. Erickson chose to involve the whole class in helping this student. He arranged with two of the students to help play a joke on the rest of the class. One accomplice was to stay on the fourth floor of the classroom building and hold the elevator while a second watched the stairwell, alerting the first when Erickson climbed the stairs to class.

The next morning Erickson arrived at the first floor elevator a few minutes before eight. In expectation of some joke perpetrated by Erickson, most members of the class were there waiting for the elevator. The medical student with the artificial leg was there also. All waited, but the elevator did not come to the first floor. In time, Erickson, who was himself handicapped from a childhood bout with polio, turned to the student with the artificial leg and said,

> "Let's us cripples hobble upstairs and leave the elevator for the able-bodies. . . ." The able-bodied waited for the elevator. Us cripples hobbled upstairs. At the end of the hour that student was socializing again—with a new identity. He belonged to the professional group: "Us cripples." I was a professor; I had a bad leg; he identified with me; I identified with him. So with that new status he regained all his outgoing ways. He was socializing at the end of the hour.[5]

The reader may have noticed by now the similarity between Erickson's approaches. In each situation he used the unusual and unexpected to begin developing rapport. Each person respected the other's world view and integrity by joining that person's life perspective. Not only did Erickson join the medical student, he also jarred the student's perspective, giving him a glimpse of life which was incompatible with his old view and easing him into a healthful change.

Jesus' encounter with the Samaritan woman illustrates the same kind of joining and jarring a person to encourage a life change (John 4). Jesus surprised her when He, a Jew, asked her, a Samaritan, for a drink of water. This unusual behavior on His part signaled a new relationship. He started by asking her for a drink and ended with giving her living water which she shared with her neighbors and friends. How did Jesus do this? After He got her attention, He intrigued her with a statement about living water. By doing this He met her at her world view: she came to draw water, a necessity probably occupying her thoughts that day. Therefore Jesus' statement about living water matched perfectly her human view and later met her spiritual need. Think back to the story about the medical student and how Erickson used surprise to develop rapport. He bridged from what the student saw as solely his problem to something they had in common. These relational approaches are strikingly similar.

LISTENING

Gaining the counselee's attention, however, is just the beginning of a life-changing relationship. "A basic requirement for successful therapy is trust."[6] Because counselees invest a large part of themselves in the counseling relationship, therapists must be trustworthy and communicate their trustworthiness to clients. The social stage in counseling is built on the client's confidence in the counselor. If that confidence falters, rapport decreases. For this reason continual maintenance of rapport is essential for change to take place, and careful listening is an important component in this process.

Listening is more than hearing. Perhaps you have poured out some important personal communication to another person who did not appear to be listening to you. When challenged, the listener repeated back what you had said, but you believed the listener had not really heard and understood your thoughts. What has to happen for listening to occur? Obviously listening is more than a physiological sensory process.[7] It involves intricate psychological procedures to process and understand sensory experience.[8] When we do not listen, we give clients the impression they are not important. In one of my counseling classes I divided the students into pairs with the assignment that one would talk for three minutes while the other did anything but pay attention. Then their roles were reversed. Some students reported they found it very difficult to even think of what to say when their counseling partner did not appear to be listening to them.

Since listening is so important, it is crucial that we consider how good listening develops. Carl Rogers was the first modern therapist to stress the importance of listening.

A . . . condition for therapy is that the therapist is experiencing an accurate, empathic understanding of the client's private world as seen from the inside. To sense the client's private world as if it were your own, but without ever losing the "as if" quality—this is empathy, and this seems essential to therapy.[9]

To gain that intimate sense of the client's internal world, we must process, not just hear, what is said.[10] Furthermore, clients must know we understand what they are saying.

Processing what is heard involves several steps. First the words themselves must be converted into our personal meanings. Then, depending on the level of communication, feeling states and the behaviors connected with those states must be accessed from memory. If we stop at this point we may or may not have an accurate understanding of what the other person has said. The next step is to repeat what was processed as our understanding of the message. The person can then correct our version or accept it as a fair representation of his or her thoughts and feelings.

Gerard Egan strongly emphasizes the importance of communicating attention with body posture.[11] Using the acronym SOLER, he collected a set of attending behaviors useful in signaling clients that they are being heard. These attending behaviors include:

1. **S**—Facing the person *squarely* rather than at an angle which would signal less involvement.
2. **O**—With arms and legs uncrossed, the counselor conveys an *open* attitude to the counselee. A closed posture signals defensiveness.
3. **L**—When two people are in a close conversation, they tend to *lean* toward each other. Such leaning signals availability or involvement.
4. **E**—Although direct *eye* contact may cause some people to feel uncomfortable, looking directly at the other's eyes is an indication that you want to be deeply involved. Shifting your gaze periodically allows your conversational partner to look away during times of deep thought.

5. **R**—Communicating a *relaxed* manner says you are at home with this person. Staying calm and comfortable yourself will let the other person know that you are composed in the conversation.

Proponents of neuro-linguistic programming (NLP), who depart from Egan in some details, also believe that the therapist's posture is important, but they believe that it should mirror that of the client. Based on the work of Milton Erickson, they found that the client senses the therapist is more in harmony when body posture is mirrored. Mirroring involves assuming a posture similar to that of the client. It also includes timing the counselor's breathing to that of the client's, or the movement of a finger or foot, for example, to the rate of breathing. These are called pacing behaviors. When the client follows the movement of the therapist, NLP holds that a deep level of rapport has been developed. However, it is important that the therapist mirror only microbehaviors, the small, unconscious behaviors like breathing rate and body position. This is done so the client does not become aware of the mirroring process, which could be construed as mimicking and would distract from what the therapist is attempting to accomplish. This kind of therapeutic attentiveness draws heavily on the counselor's ability to observe details about client behaviors.[12]

RESPONDING

Just as matching the client's nonverbal behavior helps let the counselee know you are attending, so matching on other dimensions is also critical for good rapport to develop. Three critical areas to match are cognition, culture, and content. Observing how a person internally manages and stores data is important for cognitive rapport. Cultural rapport is related to the social, racial, and family beliefs about people, the world, and life. Content rapport relates to the personal conclusions or beliefs the counselee has made as a part of learning to cooperate with others in life experiences.

COGNITION

How we manage information is important in knowing how to develop rapport. Information to be stored in long-term memory comes from all of the senses, but people tend to prefer one sense over the other four in order to retrieve memories and process information. NLP has studied behavior to help us determine which of the senses a counselee might use to process information.

Consider visual clues. These include pupil dilation and eye movements. Usually when the person looks up and to the left he or she is remembering and processing information from actual visual memory, while looking up and right is creative or constructed memory. Eyes that move toward the ears signal verbal or auditory memory recall. Looking down and left indicates verbal dialogue. Feelings or kinesthetics are accessed when the person looks down and right. When a man is asked how the ball game came out and his eyes turn down and right, he is accessing feelings to answer the question. He is proud of hitting a home run. Eyes up and to the left indicate that pictures of the ball game are used to answer the questions. Perhaps he sees himself coming across home plate. Eyes moving laterally to remember what happened would suggest he is hearing the fans' cheers (see figure 5–1).

Coupled with the eye movements are clues found in the counselee's vocabulary. People who tend to be visual construct their sentences with visual verbs, adjectives, and adverbs ("I *see* what you mean" and "I'm getting a clear picture of your

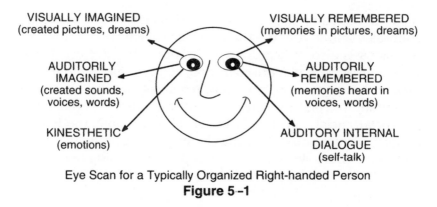

Eye Scan for a Typically Organized Right-handed Person
Figure 5–1

meaning"). Auditory and kinesthetic clues are found in the same way ("I *hear* what you say" and "I *feel* the same way"). Watching for clues from eye movements and listening to the counselee's vocabulary help the counselor to understand how the person processes information. Armed with the knowledge of how counselees process information internally, counselors can match them by using similar key words, phrases, and significant constructions. For example, if a counselee makes a visual statement (I can't see any hope), a counselor might give a visual response (I see what you mean) rather than an auditory response (I hear what you say). This matching builds rapport more quickly and is helpful for short-term counseling.

When matching counselees, flexibility is critical. If a counselor's own modality is maintained instead of adopting the counselee's, the counselee senses only a superficial communication. It is as though the two are speaking different languages. The more completely the counselor matches modalities with the client (e.g., "I get the picture, you feel . . ." and, "It sounds like you . . ."), the deeper the rapport generated between them.

CULTURE

Culture is another consideration in developing rapport. Cultural rapport considers "social and personal beliefs that are a function of national, racial, religious, and sub-cultural history and present environment."[14]

Adults feel closer to other adults, and personal communication develops more easily with age-mates. Ethnic quarters such as Chinatown and Spanish Village that exist in most large cities reflect this tendency. In order to develop thoroughly the kind of rapport that helps bring about change, the careful communicator must weigh the importance of unique cultural issues.

Gordon and Meyers-Anderson relate a story that utilized a childhood cultural belief. When staying with some friends, a woman overheard the mother and father tell their son, who feared there were monsters in his room, "There are no such things as monsters, so go back to bed." The next day the boy asked the visitor if she believed in monsters. She replied that she did but that monsters were afraid of bed covers and of milk. The child seemed relieved and reported the next morning that there were monsters in his room the previous night but that he hid beneath the covers and the monsters went away.[15]

Although the honesty of the woman in this story is questionable (a problem outside this discussion), this example contrasts the poor rapport developed by the parents who treated the child as an adult with adult understandings and the visitor who treated the child as a child with childlike understandings. Even though I would have preferred a different approach, this is a good example of considering the client's cultural beliefs and understandings.

The Bible shows other examples of cultural accommodation. Paul writes, "Oh, the depth of the riches of the / wisdom and knowledge of God! / How unsearchable his judgments, / and his paths beyond tracing out!" (Rom. 11:33). Who understands the mind of God and explains that unfathomable wisdom to human beings? God has taken that task upon Himself in the creation, revelation, and incarnation.

When I was a child, I would sit outside watching ants in long lines busily carrying foodstuffs to their nest. Sometimes there would be a rival group of red ants who would lie in ambush to capture and destroy the peaceful ants. Even though I could see what was going to happen, I could not warn the peaceful ants unless by some interference on my part. If only I could be an ant long enough to tell them of the danger—that would work. This, of course, is what God has done, in part, by sending His Son to become a man.

Yet the God-man went even further in His efforts to communicate across cultural barriers. He struggled to convey spiritual concepts in ideas and language understandable to people of His time and all time. He accommodated Himself to us culturally.

I have comforted my daughter when she thought there were creatures outside her bedroom window. I knew there were no creatures, but just telling her that gave little or no comfort. So we went into her bedroom and turned off the lights, and I asked her to show me what was frightening her. She pointed to the white window shade where the bare bushes outside her window cast shadows. What she saw was real, and it was my responsibility to help her understand what was frightening her. We raised the shades, looked at the bare branches, and noted how they were like the black shadows on the window shades. When she understood from her perspective what was causing the scary designs on the window shade, she was not as frightened and went to sleep.

I faced a different cross-cultural problem when I accepted a teaching assignment in a black community. Little did I know how much work it would take to convert to that cultural setting the same lessons I used in other places. Effective communication demanded that I accommodate to the cultural perspective of my students. Fortunately they understood and assisted me.

CONTENT

How people perceive and think about a subject is tinted not only by their cultural heritage but also by their previous experiences. Their automatic response to information has been formed into beliefs about themselves, others, and the world. For example: I'm the kind of person who likes meeting people, most people think I'm smart, I'm too short, I'm a smoker, I'm Jesus Christ. Getting at these basic beliefs is like reading between the lines, for "whenever an individual communicates with you, the content of that communication will be based on, and indicative of, certain beliefs within that person's model of the world."[16]

Consider how Jesus dealt differently with Nicodemus than He did with the Samaritan woman from Sychar. Nicodemus, as a Pharisee, was probably a rigid and compulsive person. We know from our studies of human behavior that the compulsive person tries to control the environment by setting limits and making rules or by taking control so that nothing unpredictable happens. Compulsiveness generally characterized the pharisee's approach to life. After Nicodemus's opening remark (John 3:1), Jesus shattered the interpersonal game Nicodemus was playing by breaking rules of communication. Jesus' unusual remark brought down the walls of

Nicodemus's pattern of control and started a productive conversation that ended in a positive way.

The woman of Sychar also approached Jesus with certain conclusions about life already in place (John 4). One conclusion certainly must have been that there is social safety in drawing water in the middle of the day to avoid the other women who came to draw at more favorable times. Her surprise at Jesus' approach and request for water revealed her thinking about separation between Jews and Samaritans as well as men and women. She believed in the greatness of her ancestors, among other beliefs. Jesus moved very carefully among her beliefs, using each one to turn her thinking toward His Father. No need for the same kind of shock He used to shatter Nicodemus's mind set.

Can we know other people's conclusions, when even they do not know? Shulman observes that the basic unconscious human problematic conclusions can be summarized in the following six categories:

1. Distorted attitudes about self—for example, "I am less capable than others."
2. Distorted attitudes about the world and people—for example, "Life is unpredictable."
3. Distorted goals—for example, "I must be perfect" or "I must never submit."
4. Distorted methods of operation—for example, excessive competitiveness, excessive pride, or ignoring what one doesn't wish to confront.
5. Distorted ideals—for example, "A real man is always heroic" or "The only thing worth being is a star."
6. Distorted conclusions:
    (a) pessimism—for example, "I am doomed to failure" or "Life is nothing but a trap";
    (b) "X (love, reason, money, or whatever) conquers all";
    (c) cynicism—for example, "Everyone is out only for himself" or "There is always an ulterior motive";
    (d) fanaticism—for example, "This is the best of all possible systems" or "I'm the only one who has the 'real' truth."[17]

Listening for these distortions can give the counselor an understanding of what the other person values, so interventions can be planned to use these mistaken conclusions to turn the counselee toward more productive goals.[18] An example from the life of Erickson illustrates the use of unconscious conclusions to change people.

> One summer I sold books to pay my way through college. I walked into a farmyard about five o'clock, interviewed the farmer about buying books, and he said, "Young fellow, I don't read anything. I don't need to read anything. I'm just interested in my hogs."
>
> "While you're busy feeding the hogs, do you mind if I stand and talk to you?" I asked.
>
> He said, "No, talk away, young fellow, it won't do you a bit of good. I'm not going to pay attention to you; I am busy feeding the hogs."
>
> And so I talked about my books. Being a farm boy, I thoughtlessly picked up a pair of shingles lying on the ground and started scratching the hogs' backs as I was talking. The farmer looked over, stopped, and said, "Anybody knows how to scratch a hog's back, the way hogs like it, is somebody I want to know. How about having supper with me tonight and you can sleep overnight with no charge and I will buy your books. *You like hogs.* You know how to scratch 'em the way they like to be scratched."[19]

Through experience the farmer had concluded that hogs like to have their backs scratched in a particular fashion. When he encountered someone who had reached the same conclusion, he reasoned that this was a person worth paying attention to. Erickson used the farmer's conclusion to capture his attention and gain a sympathetic ear.

A knowledge of the counselee's conclusions is critical for the counselor so they may be used to help the counselee change. Usually the counselee's conclusions are apparent and the counselor need not look for minutiae to detect them.

The way a client's disclosure of content is managed determines the level of rapport that develops.[20] After a client has disclosed information, the counselor has one of two options:

either agree with or disagree with what the client has said. For example, when the counselor disagrees with the counselee, the client is left with the choice of either agreeing with the counselor and distrusting himself or disagreeing with the counselor and damaging the trust needed for good rapport. Gordon and Meyers-Anderson comment on this dilemma.

> As individuals dedicated to the nurturance of strong, self-reliant and growing human beings we can't imagine any therapist finding either of these consequences therapeutically attractive. Confronting someone with how their model of the world is "not so" or "bad" is destructive of client-therapist trust and/or destructive of the client's trust of himself.[21]

Consider Paul's skill in joining the Athenians at their world view (Acts 17:16–34). The passage reveals that Paul was distressed over the extensive idolatry of the Athenians. He had reasoned with the Jews and God-fearing Greeks in the synagogue and with the philosophically oriented populace in the market place. The response of this latter group was contentious, but they invited him to address the Areopagus, a place where men with time to spare heard philosophical debate. This is the group to whom Paul said,

> Men of Athens! I see that in every way you are very religious. For as I walked around and observed your objects of worship, I even found an altar with this inscription: TO AN UNKNOWN GOD. Now what you worship as something unknown I am going to proclaim to you (Acts 17:22–23).

To neutralize their contention Paul had to meet them at their world view. Paul's recognition of their unknown god fit perfectly within their world view. Psychologically he turned their attention to his message by using their own perspective in such a way that they would have to deny their own theology to disagree with him. Now some may claim his results were meager, for only "a few men became followers of Paul and believed" (Acts 17:34). However, we must carefully consider the hostile atmosphere of Paul's address. The context reveals that at least some of these men were already aware of Paul's teaching and were hostile to it.

So far several essential ingredients in the development of rapport have been discussed, including using the client's vocabulary to signal that the counselor understands the client's viewpoint. Understanding is also facilitated by assessing and including elements of cultural background, such as differences among age-group levels and world cultural systems. Mirroring posture and pacing the client's breathing rate help the client feel a sense of closeness with the counselor. Rapport is also directly related to the counselor's attitudes of acceptance, understanding, and genuineness. Accepting the content of the counselee's message allows the client to feel positive about the counselor and himself or herself.

COUNSELING CAN END HERE

Carl Rogers founded the client-centered approach to counseling. Perhaps a significant reason for Rogers's success is his emphasis on the counselor-client relationship. Once people hear themselves in an accepting and warm atmosphere, they are able either to make the necessary changes or adapt their understanding sufficiently to accept life with new faith and vigor. So also we may have counselees who do not move beyond this initial stage of counseling. We cannot lose by methodically developing the social stage of therapy, for it could either end therapy right then or pave the way for additional stages to generate new and better solutions to nagging problems.

FINALLY

Most counselors recognize empathy, support, and genuineness as necessary elements of the change. Empathy captures the essence of what has been described here as rapport. Without it the counseling relationship fails to begin or to continue, and with it the relationship can result in life changes for the counselee. The *speed* with which rapport can be developed is crucial for short term counseling to proceed. The skill of creating an ambience conducive to immediate trust must be practiced faithfully by the counselor.

The second element is respect, a foundational element in Christianity. The very essence of *agape* love is a positive regard that goes beyond any human ability to value. We have that love because God has given it to us to share with others. Love is the theme of 1 John 4:7–8. Love is the motivation that drew the Lord from heaven to die for human beings, and love incites believers to minister to others as they would to the Lord Himself. This is the spirit that can make secular theory live beyond the confines of its humanistic limitations.

Genuineness in secular therapy is based on counselors' knowledge and acceptance of themselves. Although this is a good start, it cannot compare with the genuineness that comes from being known, forgiven, and accepted by God. The assets of the Christian counselor can be so much greater, but they must be realized and utilized to benefit counselees.

The realization and utilization of assets are what this book is about. We must understand, accept, and channel our clients' resources into productive ways of solving problems. Jesus started with a cup of cold water and ended with a life change that altered a Samaritan village (John 4). When the lawyers and Pharisees brought Jesus a woman caught in the act of adultery, they thought He could not answer their inquiry. Yet He did answer by using their own sense of justice to indict them, resulting in their turning away and the woman receiving forgiveness.

The creative use of resources is also illustrated in another of Erickson's cases, the treatment of a hospital patient who was so fearful that he collected bits of string to reinforce the bars on the window. Instead of rejecting or correcting the patient, Erickson joined the patient in the string-winding task. Erickson also noted that there were cracks in the floor and around the door that needed to be stuffed with newspaper. Eventually Erickson convinced the patient that the orderlies and nurses were part of the defense system available to everyone in the hospital. By suggestion, the patient's sense of security was generalized to the state board of mental health, the police, and the governor. Erickson did not reject the string-winding behavior but used it by pointing to other forms of protection that were more realistic and healthy.[22]

Erickson utilized this patient's way of handling his fear. The example is bizarre, but the principle is practical. To accept symptoms as part of the counselee's way of managing life is to demonstrate love and compassion. To do this we must see these symptoms in a way that is different than most people see them, for our understanding of symptoms must border on appreciation.[23] We must learn to see negative behaviors and descriptive terms in a positive way.[24] For example, the term "loner" is negative but can be positively recast in terms such as "private" or "personal."

A woman in therapy with me called her husband fishy, meaning he was spineless. I asked if when she said fishy, she really meant flexible; then I pointed out all the advantages of having a flexible husband: "When he comes home from work and you ask him about going out for dinner, he says, 'Sure.'" After that she did not, in my presence, call her husband fishy. By interrupting her I gained her attention, and by drawing her attention to the positive qualities of a "fishy" person, I contaminated her negative use of the word. From then on when she thought "fishy" she also was reminded of her flexible husband.

Perhaps a lesson Jesus wanted to teach His disciples as He fed the five thousand (Matt. 14:13–21) was that He could take whatever was offered and utilize it in some positive way. Those who ate that day enjoyed the Lord's provision, but it was the disciples who saw how the provision was afforded. Let's apply ourselves to developing rapport with our clients *quickly* by accepting and utilizing what they consider a problem or symptom.

Chapter 1 opened with a story about a woman who thought her lover had placed a listening device in her ear. Although odd, this was her understanding or world view at the time. If I had disagreed with her, I would have joined the ranks of all the other sensible people who had told her no listening device existed. She would have rejected me or herself. Perhaps you now can speculate on what I did to develop rapport with her.

NOTES

1. D. Gordon and M. Meyers-Anderson, *Phoenix: Therapeutic patterns of Milton H. Erickson* (Cupertino, Calif.: Meta Publications, 1981), 3.

2. R. Dayringer, *The Heart of Pastoral Counseling: Healing through relationship* (Grand Rapids, Mich.: Zondervan, 1989), 9–10.

3. C. T. Fischer, "Rapport as mutual respect," *Personnel and Guidance Journal* 48, no. 3 (1969):203.

4. Fischer, "Rapport," 203.

5. Sidney Rosen, ed., *My Voice Will Go with You: The Teaching tales of Milton H. Erickson, M.D.* (New York: Norton, 1982), 226–227.

6. See Gordon and Meyers-Anderson, *Phoenix: Therapeutic Patterns*, 35; and Dayringer, *The Heart of Pastoral Counseling*, 35.

7. R. Bolton, *People Skills: How to assert yourself, listen to others, and resolve conflicts* (Englewood Cliffs, N. J.: Prentice-Hall, 1979), 32.

8. Gerard Egan, *The Skilled Helper: A systematic approach to effective helping*, 4th ed. (Pacific Grove, Calif.: Brooks/Cole, 1990), 129.

9. Carl Rogers, *On Becoming a Person* (Boston: Houghton Mifflin, 1961), 248.

10. Egan, *The Skilled Helper*.

11. Egan, *The Skilled Helper*, 108–110.

12. A. E. Ivey and W. J. Matthews, "A metamodel for structuring the clinical interview," *Journal of Counseling and Development* 63 (December 1984).

13. David Carlson, *Counseling and Self-Esteem* (Dallas, Tex.: Word, 1988), 104.

14. Gordon and Meyers-Anderson, *Phoenix: Therapeutic patterns*, 51.

15. Ibid. p. 51.

16. Ibid. p. 42.

17. Bernard Shulman, *Contributions to Individual Psychology* (Chicago: Alfred Adler Institute, 1973).

18. Eve Lipchik, *Interviewing* (Rockville, Md.: Aspen, 1988), 36–37.

19. Rosen, *My Voice Will Go*, 59.

20. Egan, *The Skilled Helper*, 133–134.

21. Gordon and Meyers-Anderson, *Phoenix: Therapeutic patterns*, 42–43.

22. Milton H. Erickson and J. K. Zeig, "Sympton prescription for expanding the psychotic's world view," in *The Collected Papers of Milton H. Erickson*, vol. 4, ed. E. L. Rossi (New York: Irvington, 1980), 335.

23. B. P. Keeney, *Aesthetics of Change* (New York: Guilford Press, 1983), 122ff.

24. M. Edelstein, *Sympton Analysis: A method of brief therapy* (New York: Norton, 1990), 58.

PART TWO

The Method

Chapter Six

Problem Definition

IN PART ONE WE CONSIDERED SOME BASICS to effective counseling. Short-term counseling depends on the *quick* development of a positive relationship in which the counselee trusts and follows the lead of the counselor. Time is critical! In some cases individuals are not ready or able to develop a relationship so quickly. For them longer term counseling is indicated.

In the following chapters we turn to aspects of counseling which are more unique to short-term approaches. As outlined in chapter 1, these include: (1) observe the problem, (2) plan a solution, (3) adjust the plan, and (4) liberate the counselee.

People come for help because they have problems and they do not know what to do about them. At the same time they have no knowledge of how to be counselees. The counselor must let counselees know what is expected of them. After beginning to develop rapport, the counselor's next step is to assist the counselee in the development of a problem statement.[1]

Problem definition extends from the rapport-building stage of counseling. During the problem definition stage the counselor continues to use good listening skills to help the counselee spell out the parameters of the problem. These parameters easily get lost in countless variations and descriptions of events and feelings dating back further than anyone accurately remembers. To make progress, counselors need a grid or frame from which to understand counselees and to bring meaning out of chaos. The Problem Definition Grid discussed in this chapter is an adaption of Benshoff and Glosoff's six-step process for defining problems.[2]

THE PROBLEM DEFINITION GRID

The Problem Definition Grid consists of six parts based on the acronym DEFINE:

Describe the problem
Explore the problem
Find acceptable definitions
Identify ideal or future state
Note particulars
Expand into goals and implementation

Essentially, problem definition involves clarification of the complaint, description of the role of the counselee in the problem, and outlining the elements needing change. It should be noted here that, while the Problem Definition Grid progresses toward a definition of the problem, the steps themselves are not mutually exclusive or necessarily sequential.

DESCRIBE THE PROBLEM

The first step on the Problem Definition Grid is to describe the problem. Since a good definition of the problem can be essential to solving that problem, this first step is critical. To describe the problem, there are outside influences that must be understood. There are a variety of things that can confuse or obscure the problem that must be deselected. And there is a process through which the problem came to be that must be understood.

Influences on Problem Definition. People come to counseling with a history of experiences that influence the way they understand their problems. The problem bringing them to seek help began when the symptom or difficulty started; weeks, months, or years may have passed since its onset. Often the person consults with many other people about the problem before seeking the assistance of a professional. The counselor, therefore, is seldom the first person to hear the counselee's complaint. Other people may have attributed the problem to either the complainant's being bad (choosing wrong behavior) or being mad (acting or feeling in a way that shows a need to adjust to demands, illness, infirmity, etc.) or some other common sense understandings of the origin and continuity of the problem.[3] Inadvertently these friends and loved ones have played a significant role in determining how the counselee understands and handles the problem. Our job requires us to understand the problem without buying into the definitions others have appended to it.[4]

Is there a *right way* to ask for the problem statement? Absolutely! How we ask about the problem will determine how the counselee shapes the complaint, and the shape of the complaint plays a critical role in developing a solution. For example, if we allow the problem to be described as unsolvable, we have reduced the possibility of the counselee getting over the difficulties quickly. Adapting Jay Haley's description of problem definition,[5] we make the following suggestions:

1. Start with what you know from the first contact with the person. Essentially the ice has already been broken, so build on this first effort.

2. If you start with "What is the problem?" you have already categorized the counselee's situation as a problem. Do you want what is happening defined as a problem? Such a definition may be more of a problem than the original difficulty.

3. You can personalize your request by asking "What is it you want from me?" In order to answer this inquiry the counselee must formulate the problem and decide how

or what the counselor is to accomplish. Such a request requires a higher level of thinking which could lead to the counselee's actually solving the problem.

4. "What changes do you want?" shifts the focus to problem behaviors which must be changed.

5. A vague question like "Why are you here?" does not predispose the counselee to answer in a certain way and allows for the maximum amount of counselee input into the problem definition. Haley suggests when dealing with families that vagueness allows for the greatest expression of personal point of view. Part of the process of getting the problem defined is the selection of the problem to be considered first.

The counselee's beliefs about life provide another important influence on the definition of the problem. These beliefs include presuppositions and conclusions, a kind of secular theology which has developed from the beginning of life.[6] These beliefs govern not only the viewing of life but also the doing of life.

Confusing the Definition of the Problem. The problem definition stage can be confusing and many counselors lose their sense of direction.[7] In part, this confusion comes as the counselee attempts to relate several difficult–to–understand events including a number of facts and people. Listening to a counselee's problem description can be a lot like reading a long, involved novel. Another reason for this loss of direction comes from the counselee's attempt to report several problems of varying levels of intensity and discomfort. The counselor must attempt to narrow the selection to one problem at a time.[8] This gives focus to the counseling process. In the selection of one behavior for change, counselors must consider:

1. the degree of dysfunction or the severity of the behavior (e.g., homicidal, suicidal, child abuse)

2. the level of concern on the part of the counselee

3. whether the counselee believes the problem situation can be changed

4. the degree of influence such a change would have on the total person or situation

5. how the solution of one problem will lead to the resolution of other problems

6. who will be influenced by the change.

In addition to narrowing the focus, the counselor must also keep the counselee from wandering through stories which the counselee believes relate to the problem but actually are not necessary for solving the problem. At this stage of counseling the counselor must move the counselee toward a thorough exploration of the problem.

Describe the Process. At first counselees tell a lot about what they consider problems. Not only must counselors distinguish between what can be changed and what cannot be changed, we must also differentiate between content and process. Content can range over a variety of issues and, if taken as the focus of counseling, may be very confusing for both the counselor and counselee . A discussion of the process through which the problem developed gives a more predictable outcome and includes how issues are handled. Couples may argue about any number of content issues, yet the arguments usually proceed in a patterned or predictable manner. Counseling must target, explore, and change the pattern of the problem behavior.

When people come with complaints about arguing too much they will almost certainly start to describe what they argue about. They somehow believe that the counselor will deal with these particulars. Instead of *why* they fight we need to discover *how* they fight. How does it start, what happens next, then what happens, where, and with whom present, etc.? When the helper can see and hear what happens when a fight is in progress, then sufficient information is available to proceed with counseling.

EXPLORE THE PROBLEM

Exploration, which can be expedited by getting the counselee to give at least two examples, is the process of understanding exactly what occurs when a problem is in progress. Erickson reports that he was consulted by a retired policeman, "Dick," who had several complaints including obesity, smoking, and drinking too much. In the course of counseling Erickson discovered where Dick bought his food, cigarettes, and alcohol. He lived near stores that sell these items. Whenever Dick needed food, cigarettes, or alcohol he simply went to a convenient, nearby store for them. The problem depended on the availability of the items. By carefully exploring the details of Dick's life habits, Erickson discovered the pattern of the problem: exactly how Dick maintained his problem behavior.

O'Hanlon and Wilk believe that the facts of the problem should be separated from the meanings and interpretations that have been placed on the facts.[9] Facts do not change and therefore should only be accepted and processed. The attributions or the interpretations that people place on the facts are changeable; and according to O'Hanlon and Wilk, counseling is the process of changing the changeable—changing the interpretations of facts. They recommend that the helper get a "video" description of the events of the complaint, that is, a *verbal* description of what a camcorder would see and hear. This is a powerful step in resolving a problem: a realistic mental picture reveals the pattern of the problem and allows for the separation of fact from interpretation.

For example, parents often interpret disobedience as the child expressing that he or she doesn't care for or love them. Such an interpretation looks beyond observable behavior to the inner world of motivation, a difficult area (even for the child) to understand.

Effective counselors help people understand the complaint as something they want to start doing, something they want to stop doing, or something they want to do more or less.[10] In their cognitive-behavioral model O'Hanlon and Wilk explore the behavior that needs changing so that the cognitive conclusion, which blocks more appropriate behavior, may be altered. Therapy in this model begins when the counselee understands the extent of the problem. Once enough facts are known, the counselor suggests a simple solution to the problem. Counselees usually give a reason why they cannot comply, and

Wilk then pushes the person further by asking, "Why not?" The answer to this last question yields the underlying belief or conclusion that must be changed in order for the counselee to adopt a different way of doing things.[11]

Making the problem concrete during exploration makes it much easier to solve. *What* is much easier to work with than *why*. Besides, even when we know why a problem has come about, we still have the problem of doing something different. Erickson suggests thinking about therapy backwards: start with the goal and work back to where the person is at the present. Erickson even recommends as an exercise reading a book by starting with the last chapter and reading to the beginning, guessing at the contents of each preceding chapter.

Behavioral Intervention. A student once approached me following class and asked if I would help him with a problem he had recently developed. He had begun leaving the house and then returning to check to see if he had left a window open or a burner on, and so forth. The behavior was inconvenient, and he wanted to stop it. Note that I found out *what* specifically was the trouble: this behavior could be labeled compulsive, but such a label would not help get him over the problem. Once I explored the specifics of what happened, making an intervention was easy. I told him to check all he wanted, but each time he reentered the house, he was to take off his shoes and socks at the door, proceed with his checking, and then return to the door and put on his shoes and socks before leaving. He reported checking only once after that intervention. This was a simple behavioral intervention that addressed the problem by changing the pattern that maintained the behavior. He could not reach for the doorknob without wondering whether he would have to return to check and thus have to remove his shoes and socks.

Avoid Making Assumptions. Exploring the problem means getting a clear understanding of the problem as the counselee sees it. Do not assume that your understanding is the same as that of the counselee. To do so is to court misunderstanding. In the "house-checking problem" described above, it would have been easy for me to say this is not a problem at all, and discount what the counselee considered important. It is essential to understand what the problem means to the person. This operation means carefully teasing out the facts and interpretations coupled with generous amounts of active listening.

In exploring the problem, have the counselee give an example of the troublesome situation. This lets you arrive at a concrete and specific understanding of what happens and helps you make an intervention that is appropriate and effective. Jethro's understanding of what Moses was doing (Exodus 18) was essential to the kind of successful intervention that Jethro made. Dick, the retired policeman, obviously had developed specific and overt behaviors that contributed to his smoking, drinking, and obesity. Erickson's approach in that case was to interfere with the usual patterns of self-defeating behaviors by getting Dick to take longer, arduous walks to get the ingredients necessary to maintain his problem conditions.

Recently I treated a person who complained of being overweight and of not being able to do anything effective about it. I was able to get her to agree to weigh herself daily, but she was not to do anything about her weight. Shortly after that intervention was made, she reported joining a weight loss program and successfully engaging her husband's assistance in her efforts to lose weight. Now she weighs once a week—as a part of the weight loss program—but she can always go back to tipping the scales daily, as she agreed to do.

Getting her to agree to weigh herself daily was a small but simple change based on an exploration of the pattern of the problem behavior. The assignment, which was possible and easily done, forced her to face reality daily: I have a weight problem, and I want to make a change. She did!

FIND ACCEPTABLE DEFINITIONS

The third step is to find acceptable definitions for the problem. Acceptable definitions are specific and not vague. They define the problem in appropriate language and correctly label the subject as a problem, a difficulty, or some other term that makes it real. Acceptable definitions describe problems in terms that make them solvable.

Avoiding Vagueness. Usually people with a problem describe it in vague terms leaving the counselor the responsibility of insisting on a concrete description. Vagueness can be expressed in generalizations and empty or hard to define words. Many of these generalizations will sound familiar.

1. *He always does that to me.* Rarely does anything happen "all the time." The generalization "always" defines the problem as continuous, and gives the accused no credit when doing right.

2. *She expects me to read her mind.* "Expects" is difficult to define. What exactly does she do that tells you she has certain expectations?

3. *He never helps with the kids.* "Helping" with the kids is also vague. In what specific ways would she like him to help? Also, it is unlikely he *never* helps.

4. *She never wants to have good sex.* In reading this statement, I have no idea what the complaining partner expects. What is the meaning of "good sex?" What would be different?

5. *He's such a slob.* I have known some slobs in my life, but I do not know how this person is sloppy. How would he be different if he wasn't a slob?

6. *She expects too much of me.* Who can possibly know what is "expected" here? Specifically what does she "expect" that is too much? How do you know she "expects" it?

One way of obtaining a precise understanding of the counselee's experience is illustrated by Fisch, Weakland, and Segal, who organized complaints into two categories: either the identified person is either "mad" or "bad." They illustrate these two patient positions.

Set A: "We have come in because of concern about our fifteen-year-old son. He has been having extreme *difficulty adjusting* to the *demands* of school. We believe his *underlying unhappiness* is being *expressed* in *aggressiveness* to other boys in our neighborhood, and sometimes to us. We are *fearful* that he may be headed for a more serious *breakdown.*

Set B: "We have come in because of total *frustration* in *controlling* our fifteen-year-old son. He *won't* do a *lick of work* at school, even when he *decides* to attend, and now he is *picking fights* with other kids in our neighborhood. He has gotten so *nasty* at home that we decided *we needed* some *help*."[12] (Italics are in original.)

The two sets of parents view their sons' behavior differently. How they define the problem, madness or badness, becomes critical in their effectively dealing with the problem behavior. The counselor must understand that the approach to each set of parents differs. How the counselor constructs a solution depends on the willingness of the parents, and their willingness is governed by their understanding of the problem.

Problem definition aids the counselor in understanding who or what the counselee focuses on: self, others, or problems.[13] The more people focus on themselves the narrower their world view and the less likely they are to find a solution to their problem.

Language. The role of language in problem definition is critical. Benjamin Whorf believed that language shaped personal reality. The Whorfian hypothesis was developed from his experience in studying different cultures from their language bases. For example, Eskimos have a more detailed conception of snow and consequently they have several words for snow. English speakers would not understand snow as Eskimos do because we have very few words for snow: snow, sleet, freezing rain, and some terms which are coined by local weather people. It becomes obvious from Fisch's illustration of the two views of a fifteen-year-old's behavior that the label "mad" or "bad" influences how a problem should be approached. So also the language used by the counselee regarding the problem determines what approach should be taken.

For example, consider a person who says he is jealous of the relationship his wife has with her co-workers. We generally consider jealousy a negative term and a feeling a person should not have. Whether we agree or disagree with this conclusion, how we define jealousy must be considered. The counselee comes to you because this jealous feeling, which he has shared with his wife, threatens to break up their marriage. Here the problem has been defined for the counselor before the husband makes the first contact. Such a predefinition, unless changed in the counseling room, can determine how counseling will proceed.

Our search for the appropriate language in which to couch the problem must also gauge what is acceptable and understandable to the counselee. A counselor was approached by a family whose father had been removed from the home because he had allegedly been physically abusive to the children. Specifically he would boot them in the behind when he wanted to emphasize a point. This was usually accompanied by some feelings of anger but seemingly no major loss of control on the father's part. The initial session revealed that he was a mechanic in a manufacturing facility where he repaired industrial equipment. The counselor discovered his occupational interests and that, while repairing the equipment, he would often install relief valves. When it was appropriate, the counselor talked about the importance of relief valves in life and wondered what relief valves needed to be installed in the counselee's life. Understanding the counselee's language and defining his world was an important part of getting him to see what needed to be accomplished to resolve the domestic problem.

Labeling. Occasionally, an unavoidable life event has been labeled as a problem when it is only a difficulty.[14] Again language plays an important role. Mislabeling is a danger when people use the technical language of psychology and psychiatry to describe a problem: she's schizophrenic or he's depressed. By necessity professionals use abbreviated language to represent whole clusters of psychological or physiological characteristics. They, however, understand that the different nuances for each person demand that they consider each person as an individual. Unlike the general public, mental health workers do not treat the psychologic or psychiatric labels as actual facts: there really is no such person as a schizophrenic, but there are people who display behaviors labeled as schizophrenic.

An experiment was conducted in which normal people presented themselves at a hospital where they claimed to have had a visual hallucination. After they were diagnosed as schizophrenic and assigned to a unit in the hospital, they behaved normally, and their normal behavior was interpreted as an additional sign of mental illness. For example, one person decided to keep a record of experiences in the hospital, but his keeping notes was labeled by the staff as evidence of psychotic behavior. This illustrates how language can trap any of us, even the professional, into interpreting behavior in a harmful way. This same phenomenon occurs on an everyday level and certainly can hinder the work of helping people.

To understand labeling it is critical that we acknowledge that a problem has no one definition. What appear to be definitions are diagnostic conventionalities. Therefore, the language we use in defining the problem should not only be understandable to the counselee, but it should also leave the person with a way out of the problem. Avoid defining a situation as unsolvable.

Unsolvable Problems.   Watzlawick, Weakland, and Fisch outline what they consider to be unsolvable problem definitions. The first unsolvable definition is "'More of the same' or, when the solution becomes the problem."[15] In this situation the problem results from the innocent attempt to resolve a problem; and when the solution does not work, more of the same solution is applied.

Such a problem formulation can be seen in everyday life. People attempt to solve problems by using common sense; and when common sense does not help, they apply more of the same. Take for example, the family having trouble with a rebellious teenager. Common sense dictates the need for more control and restraint, inciting the teenager to further rebellion, which, in turn, leads to a call for more control and restraint, and so the cycle goes on and on. Possibly the best sense calls for something that is not common sense in such cases.

Another definition of an unsolvable problem, also from Watzlawick et al., is "the terrible simplification," which says:

There is no problem (or, at worst, it's merely a difficulty) and anybody who sees a problem must be mad or bad—in fact, he may be the only source of whatever difficulty is admitted. That is, denial of problems and attacks on those either pointing them out or trying to deal with them go together.[16]

This type of definition is illustrated in the lives of those who have gone outside the marriage relationship to satisfy their needs for intimacy. By making a game out of something very serious, the real problem goes untreated to the ultimate demise of the marital relationship. David illustrated this by covering his sin with Bathsheba. After committing sin with her, David arranged for Uriah's death, an even more heinous sin against Uriah and God. As king, David was able to cover up and keep those who knew about his sin from bringing about a correction.

The third unsolvable definition is "the utopia syndrome." In the utopia syndrome the person looks for that perfect solution to the problem, consequently, the search becomes the problem itself. These people constantly hunt for the ideal place, state, or condition. Christians are particularly susceptible to this unsolvable trap because they believe some are called to live a perfect life in God's strength. They leave out the fact of the reality of sin, a reality God has accepted and provided for, but a reality calling for a life of humble confession and admission of imperfection.

These three conditions, "more of the same," the "terrible simplification," and "the utopia syndrome," when defined as unsolvable, lead unsuspecting people down paths strewn with the weeds of misery and disgust. Always looking but never finding, their lives dissipate into nothingness.

A problem is said to exist when there is a clearly detectable discrepancy between actual (what is) and preferred (what ought to be) conditions (Brissey & Nagle, 1971). Since no problem exists when there is no discrepancy between actual and preferred conditions, the goal of problem solving becomes the reduction or elimination of any detectable discrepancy between two conditions.[17]

Defining a problem involves making a clear distinction between what can be changed and what cannot be changed.

Counseling may need to focus on adjusting to some unchangeable condition. In cases where change can occur, counseling proceeds with an analysis of the problem situation. This should include the total response chain: the precipitating stimuli (the beliefs, or the attitudes within the person); the problem response (the pattern of the response itself); and the reinforcing stimuli, both internal and external, which follow the problem response.

What makes the situation a problem is critical in at least three instances: when the reported problem seems to be minor (is the counselee simply overly sensitive or overstating the true situation?), when the reported problem is considered by most people to be a condition of life and cannot be solved as in the death of a loved one, and when the problem is really in the domain of some other professional, such as a lawyer, physician, or banker.[18]

IDENTIFY FUTURE STATE

The fourth step on the grid is to identify the ideal or future state. This requires staying focused on the ideal and avoiding roadblocks.

Focus on the Future.   The identity of the ideal or future state, like the problem statement, must be specific and concrete and is best when framed in behavioral terms. Usually the client will describe the future state in vague and hard-to-define concepts, but it is the duty of the counselor to help identify the goal in observable terms. One way to get people to be concrete is to ask them to pretend there is a mirror in the office which reflects the way life will be when the problem is solved. Only counselees are able to see what things will be like, so they must describe to the counselor what they see happening when the problem is solved. Whatever they describe will be the direction to take in the counseling process.

Still another way to ascertain counselees' goals is to have them imagine you have a magic potion or magic wand that when applied will mean they wake in the morning without the problem. What will life be like? How will they act? Who will be different? Who will first notice the changes? These techniques, which were developed by Steve de Shazer and associates at the Brief Family Therapy Center in Milwaukee, draw out the counselee and help to change the focus from the negative events in the past and present to the positive possibilities in the future.

Much of this part of the problem definition grid will be treated in chapter 8, which focuses on goals of counseling. It is, however, important to note here that what we have divided into stages is really a "total" experience that must be appreciated from a blended perspective.

Avoid Roadblocks. People are basically problem solvers—so why aren't they solving this problem? This is another useful question to help keep the counseling process moving in a positive direction. Ask yourself, "What could possibly bring this person for counseling?"[19] How has this person functioned for twenty, thirty, forty, or more years but is now in need of counseling? What has changed so much to make the problem unbearable?

Criticism, both by self and by others, exemplifies one reason problems are not solved—perfectly good solutions can be discarded without real consideration or trial. Brainstorming, a creative activity dependent on free expression of ideas, illustrates how powerful problem solving can be. One person can develop as many ideas as a group can if criticism is left to the end of the session. At that point, workable ideas are sorted and tried.

Focusing on what life would be like after the problem is solved avoids negativism because the counselor is focusing on a positive view of the future rather than a negative understanding of the past. Eeyore, a character in the *Winnie the Pooh* children's series, sees everything through gray-colored glasses. The present *and* future do not look bright for Eeyore because he has a negative mindset. The problem solver sees the future as "anything is possible" and considers many different approaches to the same problem.

An exercise called "pie analysis" allows counselees to consider their present life patterns and problems and to discern what is needed to produce a better life in the future.[20] To do a pie analysis, ask the counselees to divide a circle into sectors according to the amount of time they spend performing and/or worrying about work, family, health, social contacts, self-care, moral and religious implications, economic factors, education, recreation, sex, and personal achievement. Then ask them to restructure the proportions according to their wishes. The difference between the two pies highlights the problem(s) to address in counseling.

NOTE PARTICULARS

It is important to learn the particulars of a problem. Buried in the details are the reasons the problem continues and the clues to making a successful change. Noting the particulars can be difficult because the counselee tends to generalize or overlook the reason(s) the problem exists and the ways the problem can be solved.

It is important in the problem definition stage to recognize that the counselee probably is or has been putting forth a reasonable effort to solve the problem. This effort needs to be appreciated and valued so that the counselee can feel good about the personal effort expended in trying to solve the problem.

Getting the particulars and sorting out the patterns of behaviors may mean sending the person home to continue experiencing the problem in order to keep a record of what is happening and report this to you later. A home visit may be necessary for the counselor to gain a full understanding of the process. Whether on site or by verbal report, the actual behaviors, words, gestures, and people associated with the problem need to be assessed and considered as part of the pattern making up the problem.

With the problem broken down into its components, and with the description of the future state clearly in the mind of the counselee and counselor, the solution may become apparent. Another obstacle, the counselee's resistance to change, will be discussed in chapter 7.

EXPAND INTO GOAL SETTING AND IMPLEMENTATION

The next natural step sets up a goal and puts into operation the necessary behaviors for meeting the goal. Proper problem definition is essential to goal setting. Motivating the counselee to make changes is critical in getting the person to start new behavior. Dinkmeyer and Losoncy specify the characteristics of the self-encouraged person who moves into life problems with confidence.[21] The characteristics of such persons, adapted for our use, are:

1. Be decisive and take responsibility.
2. Have confidence in what you think of the world.
3. Learn to think independently of others.
4. Be willing to disagree when appropriate.
5. Expect to need less power and attention.
6. Take appropriate risks.
7. Open up to consider various alternatives.

Commitment by the counselor is part of problem definition. By the end of the problem definition stage counselors must convey, with feeling and believability, that they can and want to help the counselee. Inspiring hope in the counselee is a significant step in getting the client to follow the counselor's suggestions. Conveying to counselees that you believe in their ability to overcome the problem gives them the kind of cognitive and emotional lift that generates new thoughts, feelings, and behaviors which result in change.

COUNSELING CAN END HERE

The fact that counseling can end at this stage may seem evident. If the counselee defines the problem as solvable, and if the solution is within the person's repertoire, the problem may dissolve. When the solution is not in the counselee's repertoire, the task of counseling may turn to helping the person develop new skills and practice new behaviors. In such a situation the counselor becomes a coach who trains and encourages the counselee.

A manicurist came to counseling complaining that she was obsessed with having different types of diseases. She reported hearing her customers talk about physical complaints and soon experienced the same symptoms. This case was easily resolved by explaining to her how psychology students, when reading pathology textbooks, often find themselves experiencing every problem they read about. This made sense to her, and I went on to say that I thought she was suggestible, easily impressed when she heard stories. This understanding she accepted also. Now she had only to pay attention to what was happening around her and ignore the subjective impressions she tended to develop as she listened to the physical complaints. Since this part of her therapy was accomplished in the first session, we were able to move on immediately.

FINALLY

This chapter has addressed the problem definition stage of short-term counseling. The basic principle behind problem definition is a clear, objective, and solvable definition of the problem. Typically, people are vague about what bothers them and unclear about what life would be like in a problem-free future. Helping counselees be specific and concrete is hard work, but it pays high dividends in solutions. Counselor success at this stage hinges on creativity and flexibility. Flexibility includes the ability to see the problem from different perspectives and to create solutions for unique predicaments. Flexibility in perspective means that labels are arbitrary meanings we ascribe to sensory data and that these labels can and must be shifted to allow for solutions.

NOTES

1. D. S. Gentner, "A brief strategic model for mental health counseling," *Journal of Mental Health Counseling* 13 (1991), 1.

2. James Benshoff and Harriett Glosoff, "Getting Clear: A model for problem definition in counseling," *American Mental Health Counselors Association Journal* 7, no. 4 (October 1985), 189.

3. R. Fisch, J. H. Weakland, and L. Segal, *The Tactics of Change: Doing brief therapy* (San Francisco: Jossey-Bass, 1982), 89ff.

4. Gentner, "A brief strategic model," 58–68.

5. Jay Haley, *Problem-solving Therapy: New strategies for effective family therapy* (San Francisco: Jossey-Bass), 19–20.

6. Jean Piaget, the noted developmentalist, discusses such belief-like cognitive structures.

7. Wayne Dyer and John Vriend, *Counseling Techniques That Work* (American Association for Counseling and Development, 1988), 35–36.

8. Long-term counseling deals with several problems over an extended time period. A distinction of short-term counseling is the narrow and strategic selection of only one problem. A strategic problem is related to several other problems which will dissolve as the strategic problem is resolved.

9. Bill O'Hanlon and James Wilk, *Shifting Contexts: The generation of effective psychotherapy* (New York: Guilford, 1987), 19–21.

10. O'Hanlon and Wilk, *Shifting Contexts*, 72.

11. O'Hanlon and Wilk, *Shifting Contexts*, 44–45.

12. Fisch, Weakland, and Segal, *Tactics of Change*, 89ff.

13. A. E. Ivey and N. Gluckstern, *Basic Influencing Skills: Participant manual* (Amherst, Mass.: Microtraining Associates, 1976), 52–57.

14. Charles Huber and Barbara Backlund, *The Twenty Minute Counselor: Transforming brief conversations into effective helping experiences* (New York: Continuum, 1991), 21–23.

15. Paul Watzlawick, James Weakland, and Richard Fisch, *Change: Principles of problem formation and problem resolution* (New York: Norton, 1974), 31.

16. Watzlawick, Weakland, and Fisch, *Change*, 40.

17. Philip Browning and William Wright, "A technique for problem identification in rehabilitation," *Rehabilitation Counseling Bulletin* 17, no. 1 (September 1973), 30.

18. Fisch, Weakland, and Segal, *Tactics of Change*, 74.

19. In a personal communication Jim Wilk reported asking himself what could bring a person who has gotten this far in life to seek counseling. Such an attitude allows the counselor to keep a fresh perspective of the client.

20. F. Kanfer and B. Schefft, *Guiding the Process of Therapeutic Change* (Champaign, Ill.: Research Press, 1988), 185–86.

21. S. Dinkmeyer and L. E. Losoncy, *The Encouragement Book: Becoming a positive person* (New York: Prentice-Hall, 1987), 292–98.

Chapter Seven

Attempted Solutions

So far we have developed a warm and accepting atmosphere in counseling where the counselee and counselor can co-create the problem definition. In this chapter we consider the attempted solutions which tell us a lot about what perpetuates the problem.

PLANNING A SOLUTION

From the start, developing humans find answers to problems in a trial-and-error fashion or by watching others. As we grow older we continue to use the methods that work best for us; they become strong by repetition.

It is not difficult to see how a person's solution can become the problem. When faced with a new difficulty, people use tried-and-true solutions. When these solutions do not work, instead of trying something new, people tend to increase their efforts using the same old solution. This monomethod of solving problems then becomes a problem in itself.

It is important to the therapeutic alliance that counselors avoid criticizing attempted solutions and appreciate them as an indication of the person's strengths.[1] When the counselor discovers a strength and brings it to the attention of the counselee, a sense of comradeship develops which furthers the counseling relationship and process. Finding a strength also improves the counselor's attitude toward the counselee. It is easy for counselors to generalize or acquire a negative frame for the counselee; finding strengths prevents the negative frame from wrecking the therapeutic alliance.

Repackaging an existing solution may be an effective way of giving the counselee a way out of the predicament. The collective wisdom of neighbors, friends, and relatives may be reflected in the counselee's attempted solutions. Within them is a cache of possible solutions. When understood and applied differently these solutions may transform the problem situation.

RESISTANCE

Probably the most important benefit of learning the counselee's attempted solutions is to discover how the counselee will resist progress. Resistance, a common factor in all problems, "refers to any behavior on the part of the client that appears to be getting in the way of the desired therapeutic outcome."[2] Even though resistance does not make sense—you might expect that if a person were hurting enough, that person would be glad to do anything to stop the hurt—the effective counselor knows about resistance, accepts it as a fact, and uses it to help the counselee get over the problem.

Although resistance is usually viewed from the counselor's perspective, counselees have their own perspectives.[3] Resistance may be seen as the link in a chain of coping behaviors that starts with patterns of successful responding and continues with predispositions to act.[4] From birth, children adapt to the world around them. Patterns of responding make life more efficient and therefore we repeat them frequently.

If people were not behaving in unproductive repetitive patterns, they would not be in the counselor's office. When people are able to try out alternative solutions, they often hit upon a way to solve the problem.

Resistance is a metaphorical message about fear, anger, loneliness, etc., which limits the counselee's ability to cooperate or conquer the distressing problem. Wild animals, when startled, tend to freeze before they mobilize for action. In a similar fashion people entangle themselves in situations that do not yield to their usual methods of coping. The result is uncertainty and high levels of anxiety. When counselees freeze because of anxiety, it is often interpreted as resistance. The counselor, especially in the beginning of counseling, should attempt to help the counselees relax and trust the counselor's ability to help.

People tend to raise their level of anxiety by asking themselves questions as they come for help. Kanfer and Schefft have formulated five questions which reflect counselees' concerns:

1. What will it be like if I change?
2. How will I be better off if I change?
3. Am I able to change?
4. What will it cost to change?
5. Can I trust this therapist and setting to help me get there?[5]

Counselors need to take a benevolent attitude toward such questioning and be prepared to address these fear-engendering inquiries by the level of rapport they develop, the confidence they exude, and the patience they communicate to their counselees.

From the counselor's perspective it is easy to interpret resistance as personal rejection.[6] When counselees do not keep appointments, refuse to honor the counseling contract, keep relevant information to themselves, seem not to understand the counselor's comments, and don't relinquish old expectations or behaviors, the counselor, out of frustration, may blame the counselee for blocking progress in counseling.[7] Of course, a large measure of the responsibility is the counselee's burden, but the facilitating role of the counselor cannot be overlooked.

One reason for resistance may be that the counselee does not own the counselor's goal. Research suggests that people do not have to create their own goals, but they do have to take ownership of a goal if they expect to achieve it.[8]

In turn, how the counselor utilizes a counselee's interference may make the difference between success and failure in the consulting room. How counselors view resistance may make a huge difference in how they deal with it. As Lynn Hoffman says, "resistance or opposition might better be called persistence."[9] When we think of the counselee's resistance in a positive light, we release within ourselves great creative potential to deal with resistance as well as the exigencies of the problem situation. As long as we think of resistance in a negative way, we hamper its resolution and the progress of therapy.

Resistance should not only be viewed from the counselor's perspective; it must also be seen as an objective reality evident to any onlooker. First, clues from the initial contact may warn of resistance. Difficulty with making the appointment, including problems with setting the time and day or where to meet, may suggest that the counselee wants to manage the therapeutic relationship from the beginning. Second, noncompliance is an important clue. Erickson often, after the first interview, gave a counselee a simple but somewhat inconvenient assignment to accomplish. If the counselee complied, therapy would continue; if not, further counseling was in jeopardy. Steve de Shazer assumes that counselees have their own ways of doing things and that the counselor, when encountering resistance, does not understand the counselee well enough. For both Erickson and de Shazer noncompliance provides valuable information about the counselee's approach to life, permitting counselors to make adjustments in how they work with the counselee in the future.

TYPES OF RESISTANCE

The counselor is wise to distinguish among different types of resistance. Egan understands resistance to be the result of counselor coercion.[10] Erickson asks, "How often is resistance the result of the therapist's intruding upon intimate memories, intimate ideas?"[11]

While resistance is the client's response to coercion, *reluctance* is a milder form of resistance resulting generally from fear of or unwillingness to change. Egan cites several reasons for reluctance: fear of intensity, lack of trust, fear of disorganization, shame, and fear of change.[12] Reluctance, a factor of the cost of change, is felt by almost everyone to some degree when considering change.

> Reluctant clients are more likely to seem unsure of what they want, talk about only safe or low-priority issues, benignly sabotage the helping process by being overly cooperative, set unrealistic goals and then use them as an excuse for not working, not work very hard at changing their behavior, and be slow to take responsibility for themselves.[13]

Demoralization, another concept associated with lack of progress in counseling, may look like resistance. It consists of "subjective incompetence, loss of self-esteem, alienation, hopelessness (feeling that no one can help), or helplessness (feeling that other people could help but will not)."[14] Demoralization is negatively correlated with optimism.[15]

Resistant counselees react to the counselor's intrusion into their personal knowledge, experience, and feelings. Reluctance is not so much a reaction to intrusion as it is a general response to any change. Most people are reluctant when they know that change is imminent. Reluctance should lessen as the counselees gain confidence in the counselor and themselves. Resistance, however, does not decrease until the counselor reduces the level of coercion. And demoralization seems to touch on the counselee's level of hope and confidence. We often characterize a football team that has experienced a resounding loss by using such words as demoralization, a loss of hope, even despair. Demoralization is a reaction to the reversals and disappointments of life. It is possible, of course, for a counselor to serve as a disappointment and thus a demoralizing agent.

Let's consider biblical examples of reluctance, resistance, and demoralization. The story of the rich young ruler illustrates reluctance. When told to sell all that he had and give to the poor, he responded by going "away sad, because he had great wealth" (Matt. 19:22). Even though the rich man wanted to improve his life, he was not willing to make the necessary changes to accomplish his desire. The ruler asked for advice from Jesus, but he was reluctant to change because it meant giving away his wealth.

In another example, from the Acts of the Apostles, Agrippa represents people who are resistant. When confronted with the truth of the gospel, Agrippa pushed the truth away from himself by saying, "Do you think that in such a short time you can persuade me to be a Christian?" (Acts 26:28). Paul was persuasive and Agrippa was resistant. From a human perspective Paul depicts the demoralized person in 2 Corinthians (1:8b), "We were under great pressure, far beyond our ability to endure, so that we despaired even of life."

CAUSES OF RESISTANCE

Why do people refuse help when it is so desperately needed? The literature proposes three main causes of resistance in therapeutic subjects: personal security, personal value, and personal uniqueness.[16]

PERSONAL SECURITY

The need for personal security deeply influences the lives of all human beings. The power of the familiar is so great that people will endure extreme discomfort rather than change. The obsessive counselee is a good example of such an imbalance. The false security of perfectionism is so important to this person that, even though it causes severe pain, he or she feels insecure without it. Obsessive persons would rather accept the known pain of failing to meet their goal of perfection than seek real security. Counselees will actually say they know that the symptom is senseless and should be abandoned, but the symptom is so familiar, and thus comforting, that they will not let it go.

Obsessing is not the only way counselees maintain their level of comfort. Secure feelings also develop around patterns of behavior that provide individuals with a sense of predictability and rightness and the feeling that they are free from the unexpected.[17] Such reliability is not abnormal in itself, but may become abnormal when the counselee becomes rigid and inflexible in his or her behavior patterns.

An example of such rigidity is the behavior of a man named Chris who would not sit in a restaurant unless his back was against a wall. Somehow Chris had developed a sense of security connected with the wall-to-his-back sitting behavior. During treatment Chris was challenged to try different sitting behaviors. His friends, who knew about his penchant for such protective sitting, were willing to support Chris as he tried new behaviors, quickly resolving the self-protective actions.

Resistance may be a response to stimuli in the environment, competing with the desired change. But changes in the environment may be necessary in order to facilitate new behavior. Skinner has demonstrated, through teaching animals extraordinary behavior, that a reinforcer following a behavior will encourage that behavior to happen again. In a sense we cooperate with the environment. Resistance, therefore, may be reduced by changing the reinforcers in the environment in order to bring about an effective solution. For example, putting highly desirable food, a reinforcer, out of sight reduces the overeater's persistance. To make such changes the counselor should establish how each element of the problem environment contributes to the maintenance of the symptomatic thought, feeling, or behavior. This may be confirmed by asking, "What happens first? Then what happens? And next?"

Essentially, resistance provides a sense of security which, when lost, may create such anxiety that the counselee willingly lives with the symptomatic thoughts, feelings, and behaviors rather than lose the sense of security. The counselor must provide support while the counselee changes. To overcome resistance the counselor must help counselees find ways to achieve greater levels of confidence and security.

PERSONAL VALUE

The second cause of resistance is the need for personal value. Counseling may create resistance because people perceive it as humiliating, known to be for "crazy" people. Overcoming this stigma is pivotal in the early stages of counseling. If counselees accept the idea of counseling as a tutorial relationship and learning as a lifelong process, then there is a good chance they will feel better about the counseling process. It is also important for them to be convinced of the confidential nature of the counseling relationship. Some counselees feel they must tell other people about their being counseled. Convincing people that they need not tell anyone may also help relieve the counseling stigma.

PERSONAL UNIQUENESS

The third major cause of resistance stems from the fear of the loss of uniqueness. From childhood days people learn to control their environment in such a way that they feel good about themselves. Violating this sense of uniqueness invites resistance. When people sense that their personal freedom is threatened, they display resistance in an effort to restore the freedom.

Resistance can mean people tend to assert their sense of self-determination by doing the opposite of what is suggested to them.[18] Resistance may be seen as a function of personal independence from all authority, even God's authority, as illustrated in the fall of Adam and Eve. Humans seem bent on being independent and godlike. Many people interpret this as freedom from responsibility.

Egan believes that coercion, either perceived or real, is a key factor in client resistance.[19] When the counselor moves with the counselee in such a way that the counselee's beliefs, attitudes, and habits are utilized to bring about change, there is little resistance. When encountering resistance, counselors must ask themselves, "How am I coercing or pushing this counselee?" Screening our own behaviors helps keep counselees from pushing us out of the therapeutic process.

Resistance may be traced to the counselee's desire to maintain some control and thus uniqueness in life. Even if the symptom is painful it may seem more unnerving to change patterns that would result, at least temporarily, in uncertainty. Or resistance may be a message from a counselee who lacks knowledge, expertise, or other skills necessary during the therapeutic process.[20]

Resistance "is frequently the client's attempt at self-protection from a world that is too overwhelming or frightening to face directly."[21] Human beings are constantly bombarded with stimuli calling for adjustments that may, if not screened, throw them into confusion and system failure. Considered from this perspective, resistance becomes a protective measure counselees take to manage the amount of stress in their lives. Resistance, then, is something like a peel on an apple or orange, or human skin, keeping out any unnecessary changes not in the best interest of the counselee.

The involuntary client has a particularly thick skin, making him or her the epitome of resistance. Forced into counseling by the law, school, spouse, or others, involuntary clients may feel coerced into a relationship for which they see little reason. Furthermore, the counseling relationship for the involuntary client may be seen (whether correctly or not) as a form of punishment. Although difficult to convert to compliance, involuntary counselees may become cooperative when they realize that the counselor is on their side and that any changes will be in their best interests.

Whether the resistance relates to the counselee's needs for security, personal value, or sense of uniqueness, it is a fact of counseling. The result of the interchange between the counselee's resistant behavior and the counselor's determination depends to a large extent on how the counselor views the resistance. If taken personally, the chances of working through it are much less than if the resistance is taken as a normal aspect of handling the demands of life. Thinking of resistance as persistence allows counselors to take a different attitude toward the counselee. This could initiate a whole new outcome to the counseling.

WAYS OF DEALING WITH RESISTANCE

Resistance "should be respected rather than regarded as an active and deliberate or even unconscious intention to oppose the therapist."[22] Dealing with the counselee's resistance means respecting the total person. Remember, resistance is part of the reason the counselee is in your office. The counselee's style of opposing may reveal the overall problem and thereby assist the counseling process.[23] However, if the counselor takes the resistance as a personal rejection or begins to see the counselee as an adversary, then the therapeutic relationship is in serious jeopardy. Keeping a positive attitude toward counselees is absolutely essential if we are to gain ground in the process of helping others change.

GENERAL PRINCIPLES

When the pain of change exceeds the gain of change, the counselee may exhibit negative or anxious thoughts. Cormier and Cormier recommend the exploration of fantasies, expectations, and fears.[24] This exploration helps relieve the counselee's pain, and sometimes allows for the correction of mistaken ideas, information, or beliefs. High levels of support and small changes help the counselee start the change process and pave the way for further change. Use experience to ameliorate the pain of change. A tentative explanation for the counselee's behavior may also meet and change resistance.

Resistant behavior is so complex that it is impossible to formulate an intervention for each behavior; however, we may use the problem-solving model to facilitate the forward movement of the counselee.[25] Ask yourself, "What is the present situation? What would be a better situation?" Brainstorm how to get from the current situation to the preferred one, make sure the counselee owns the goal and action steps, and help the counselee to inaugurate the changes necessary to promote forward movement.

Forward movement may also be hampered if the counselee holds on to the past. Letting go of the past is a critical part of moving on.

In order to take a step forward in one's own behalf, one must also be willing to leave something behind. . . . Values about stability and commitment, fear of the unfamiliar, fear of success, fear of failure, secondary gain issues, and a host of other explanations have surfaced as reasons for why people, even those in pain might drag their feet in moving on.[26]

Consequences that follow a behavior also encourage counselees to drag their feet. Happy or pleasant consequences following resistant behavior assure that the behavior will recur. It is our job to help the counselee find alternate behaviors that will produce more pleasant consequences than the old persistent behaviors afforded. Training a child to use eating utensils properly must be followed with appropriate praise assuring that the new behavior is more likely to recur.

Our consideration of principles for dealing with resistance includes those appropriate for mild resistance and those useful for stubborn cases of resistance. Of course any distinction reflecting the differences between simple and difficult cases of resistance is purely arbitrary and need not be considered an absolute reflection of reality. Sometimes what appears to be simple resistance is very difficult to deal with, while complicated cases of resistance may yield to rather brief and simple interventions.

TECHNIQUES FOR MILDER FORMS OF RESISTANCE

It is vital to build into the counseling process techniques for dealing with resistance. The more of these techniques a counselor includes in the interview, the more results he or she can expect. The mnemonic device EASE will facilitate remembering the techniques for dealing with mild resistance. These are:

Cultivate *expectancy*
Develop a strong therapeutic *alliance*
Teach *skills*
Explain change in terms of counselee behavior

Expectancy prepares the way to deal with resistance.[27] For weeks or months the person has been trying to feel better or to find a way to solve the problem. When people come to the first interview they are likely to be very discouraged and hopeless in their outlook. Changing that outlook means we have to deal with their sense of expectancy by helping them be successful.[28]

One approach gives counselees assignments they can't help but do successfully. Another asks them to keep a record of their symptoms.

Developing a strong therapeutic *alliance* was covered in chapter 5 where we discussed the social stage, including rapport. It is important, however, to note again that the therapeutic alliance needs constant tending throughout the counseling process. Resistance can be managed by building such a level of rapport that counselees abandon the resistant behavior or attitude.[29] They must believe that the counselor is on their side and that the counselor can be trusted to encourage any efforts they make to deal with the problem.

Skill training is important because the counselee's resistance may result from a lack of skill or knowledge. People in therapy may be tired of what is happening but not know how to change. The best resolution in this case is specific instructions or skill training. Lack of assertiveness is an excellent example of such a deficiency. People often withdraw into themselves or strike out aggressively because they do not know how to communicate their thoughts and feelings effectively. For those who need assertiveness training, this lack of skill could easily be interpreted as resistance.

Or, resistance may be an integrity statement which says, "I am whole, I am to be respected, I am able to solve my problems." Social psychological research reveals that change attributed to self is more likely to be maintained than change attributed to external agents.[30] Getting people to participate in formulating a solution to the problem is an important way of attributing success to their efforts. Of course, it is also critical that, when change does occur, people hear their counselors *explain* the improvement as the result of the counselee's new behavior.

In summary, counselors may stem simple resistance by building *expectancy*, maintaining the therapeutic *alliance*, improving *skills* and increasing knowledge, and *explaining* improvement in terms of the counselee's changed behavior. But what methods are useful when we face stubborn resistance?

TECHNIQUES FOR PERSISTENT RESISTANCE

Generally, even stubborn resistance needs to be appreciated as a unique expression of the counselee's individuality. No doubt the common sense approach to dealing with resistance is to confront it, working through the reasons for the resistance. As noted above, resistant patterns may reveal the counselee's style, affecting life to the point that the style needs changing. Confronting the resistance may invite more resistance because the counselee entrenches to maintain a sense of integrity and self-control. Other indirect ways of dealing with persistent resistance are probably better used first, with direct confrontation saved for a last attempt. Utilization, reframing, paradox, and pattern interruption are indirect measures of dealing with resistance.

Utilization.   Dealing with resistance is partially summed up in Erickson's concept of utilization.[31] Utilization employs resistance to generate a solution. Erickson used this approach to help the hospitalized patient who, for more security, wound string through the bars on the window in his room. When Erickson joined the patient by helping wind the string in the bars, he took over the defensive action and guided it in a direction which proved healthier for the patient.[32] Erickson avoided resistance by going along with the patient and then focused him on other more legitimate forms of security. Always try "to use whatever the patient brings into the office. If they bring . . . opposition . . . , be grateful for that . . . opposition. Heap it up in whatever fashion they want you to—really pile it up."[33] This approach makes it difficult for the counselee to be resistant because the counselor forces the symptom on to the counselee.

Let counselees have their resistance. If the counselor tries to take the resistance away, the counselee will likely hold onto it even more tenaciously. Erickson illustrated such an approach with the following story.

> If a farmer with prime hunting land on his farm puts up a "No trespassing" sign, the hunters will sneak onto his land to hunt. If, however, the farmer meets with the hunters and tells them that they can hunt on a specific parcel of ground, they are much more likely to remain in that area.[34]

Utilize resistance. Channel it into the process of recovery. Resistance is a part of the motivation that counselees bring to the consulting room. "Oppositions . . . constituting a part of the problem can be utilized by enhancing them and thereby permitting the patient to discover, under guidance, new ways of behavior favorable to recovery."[35] Imagine yourself with a resistance such as your counselee has. Now think of what would help you to sense the problem situation differently. How can your resistance be used to get you to see the situation in a new way? Work your answer into the counselee's problem situation.

Reframing. Resistance may be reframed as the counselee's effort to help the counseling process. A reframe is possible when a behavior, feeling, or object is legitimately a member of two categories at the same time. For example, Watzlawick reframes teenage rebellion as a deep-seated fear of growing up. The teenager can then disagree only by not being rebellious. Changing labels or reframing is possible because language is actually a metaphorical construction placed on the input of our senses. (For a further discussion of constructs, see chapter 3.)

Say what you want the counselee to hear, but put it in a frame of not saying it. For example, you could say, "If you were older, I would say . . ."[36] This technique allows the counselor to say what needs saying with less chance of raising the counselee's defenses. Getting the counselee to listen without automatically dismissing the content of the message is crucial in developing therapeutic change.

Paradox. Circumscribe resistance by predicting that the counselee will have a certain reaction to what you are about to say. For example, "You will probably disagree with me, but I think . . ." Typically, the counselee will not have or will deny having the response you have predicted. In a similar way, resistance may be utilized by asking for more of it. This paradoxical technique forces the counselee to oppose the counselor and move in a healthier direction.[37]

The counselor may get around this problem by asking the counselee not to report any progress under any circumstances even though he or she is getting better. Any further complaints are interpreted as compliance with the command not to report any improvement.[38] Wilk identifies this technique as a way of jamming the communication channels between the counselee and the counselor in such a way that the counselee can only go along.[39]

Some counselees have negative or uncertain attitudes about the outcome of counseling. These are best handled by agreeing with their pessimism in an empathic way rather than disagreeing and causing them to entrench themselves in a position opposite to that of the counselor. Disagreeing with the counselee can only lead the counselee to either a distrust of self or a distrust of the counselor.[40]

Pattern Interruption. Resistance may be managed better if the old pattern of behavior is scrambled before the introduction of any new behavior. Pattern interruption prepares the client to choose a new way of behaving that may lead to new thoughts and feelings. This can be compared to being forced to take a new way home from work, only to discover something pleasant along the way. There is always the possibility of new experiences which end in different thoughts and feelings.

THERAPY CAN END HERE

By the time people come for counseling, whatever options they previously had have usually failed. In other words, counselees do not know what to think or do about their problems. Resistance to any new behavior is common in all of us, but resistance plays an important role in keeping counselees from trying innovative avenues to reach new destinations and better health. If counselors effectively meet resistance in a way that encourages counselees to spontaneously try new ways of thinking and behaving, change is likely to occur at this point. Counseling could end here, but that all depends on the skill of the counselor and the persistence of the counselee to stay with an unhealthy frame of mind, a debilitating feeling, or a crippling behavior.

FINALLY

Chapter 7 has focused primarily on resistance as a part of drawing the attempted solutions from counselees. It is important to remember that attempted solutions are also useful for finding solutions that have worked at one time but are not now in the counselee's service. As emphasized, the counselee has developed many strengths which may be blocking the path to the solution that will really make a difference. Reviewing attempted solutions and recognizing strengths also enhances the therapeutic relationship. Reviewing attempts is a useful phase in helping people. Make regular use of it.

NOTES

1. Charles Huber and Barbara Backlund, *The Twenty Minute Counselor: Transforming brief conversations into effective helping experiences* (New York: Continuum, 1991), 48–49.

2. Yvonne Dolan, *A Path with a Heart: Ericksonian utilization with resistant and chronic clients* (New York: Bruner/Mazel, 1985), *xvi*.

3. Jay Efran, M. Lukens, and R. Lukens, *Language, Structure, and Change: Frameworks of meaning in psychotherapy* (New York: Norton, 1990), 188.

4. Michael Yapko, *When Living Hurts: Directives for treating depression* (New York: Bruner/Mazel, 1988), 62.

5. F. Kanfer and B. Schefft, *Guiding the Process of Therapeutic Change* (Champaign, Ill.: Research Press, 1988), 129–31.

6. Carol Anderson and Susan Stewart, *Mastering Resistance: A practical guide to family therapy* (New York: Guilford, 1983), 2.

7. Anderson and Stewart, *Mastering Resistance*, 1.

8. Kanfer and Schefft, *Guiding the Process*, 147–48.

9. In Anderson and Stewart, *Mastering Resistance*, 4.

10. Gerard Egan, *The Skilled Helper: A systematic approach to effective helping*, 4th ed. (Pacific Grove, Calif.: Brooks/Cole, 1990), 20.

11. Milton H. Erickson, "Hypnotic approaches to therapy," *American Journal of Clinical Hypnosis* 20 (1977b), 34.

12. Egan, *Skilled Helper*, 171–72.

13. Ibid. p. 171.

14. J. Frank, "Therapeutic Components Shared by All Psychotherapies," in *Cognition and Psychotherapy*, ed. M. J. Mahoney and A. Freeman (New York: Plenum, 1985), 56.

15. Kanfer and Schefft, *Therapeutic Change*, 125–26.

16. See Anderson and Stewart, *Mastering Resistance, 24, 30;* Egan, *The Skilled Helper*, 170; and Dolan, *A Path with a Heart*, 9.

17. Anderson and Stewart, *Mastering Resistance*, 24.

18. J. W. Brehm, *Response to Loss of Freedom: A theory of psychological resistance* (Morristown, N. J.: General Learning Press, 1972).

19. Egan, *The Skilled Helper*, 170.

20. Yapko, *Depression*, 89.

21. Dolan, *A Path with a Heart*, 9.

22. Milton H. Erickson, "The 'surprise' and 'my-friend-John' techniques of hypnosis: minimal cues and natural field experimentation," *American Journal of Clinical Hypnosis* 6 (1964), 299.

23. Anderson and Stewart, *Mastering Resistance*, 2–3.

24. William Cormier and L. Sherilyn Cormier, *Interviewing Strategies for Helpers: Fundamental skills and cognitive behavioral interventions* (Pacific Grove, Calif.: Brooks/Cole, 1991), 553.

25. Egan, *The Skilled Helper*, 98–99.

26. Yapko, *Depression*, 91.

27. Anderson and Stewart, *Mastering Resistance*, 4.

28. S. Spencer and J. Adams, *Life Changes: Growing through personal transitions* (San Luis Obispo, Calif.: Impact Publishers, 1990), 22.

29. Dolan, *A Path with a Heart*, 68–69.

30. Anderson and Stewart, *Mastering Resistance*, 9.

31. In Egan, *The Skilled Helper*, 174–175.

32. Dolan, *A Path with a Heart*, 10.

33. Milton H. Erickson and E. Rossi, *Experiencing Hypnosis* (New York: Irvington, 1981), 16.

34. Jay Haley, *Conversations with Milton H. Erickson, M.D.*, vol. 3, *Changing Children and Families* (New York: Norton, 1985), 29.

35. Milton H. Erickson and J. K. Zeig, *The Collected Papers of Milton H. Erickson on Hypnosis*, vol. 4, ed. Ernest L. Rossi (New York: Irvington, 1980), 48.

36. Paul Watzlawick, *The Language of Change: Elements of therapeutic communication* (New York: Basic Books, 1978), 145, 151.

37. Watzlawick, *Language of Change*, 145, 150.

38. Ibid. p. 149–50.

39. James Wilk, "Ericksonian therapeutic patterns: A pattern which connects," in *Ericksonian Psychotherapy, vol. 4, Clinical Applications*, ed. J. K. Zeig (New York: Bruner/Mazel, 1985), 220–27.

40. D. Gordon and M. Meyers-Anderson, *Phoenix: Therapeutic patterns of Milton H. Erickson* (Cupertino, Calif.: Meta, 1981), 42.

Chapter Eight

Goal Setting: Adjusting the Solution

A FRIEND AND I RECENTLY AGREED to have lunch but neglected to designate a restaurant. Although we often went to the same place, I knew my friend also liked another restaurant. I looked in the parking lots of both restaurants and went into each before I found him. Of course, we should have agreed on the restaurant ahead of time. Likewise, no one would go to an airport and get on the first airplane available or buy a ticket to just anywhere. We first decide on a destination. Setting goals is such an integral part of life that we usually take it for granted. It makes sense, then, that when we enter into a therapeutic relationship we set a goal for counseling. This may not be easy.

One of the main reasons we fail to establish goals lies in the assumptions of the counseling model guiding the counselor. Therapies emphasizing the development of human potential (i.e., client-centered psychotherapy) believe that people will grow and heal if given a healthy environment. Therefore, the counselor's responsibility is to provide acceptance and reflective listening but no guidance. The challenge of motivating people to describe where they want to go is another reason counselors avoid goal setting. Usually people know what they do not want, but are uncertain about what they actually desire. Counselors sometimes do not know how to set goals in counseling, and this keeps the counseling process from going in a purposeful direction. This chapter includes an overview of goal setting, and discusses the importance of goal setting, hindrances to goal setting, characteristics of goals, formulation of workable goals, and implementation of goals.

OVERVIEW OF GOAL SETTING

Goals are descriptions of what we want to achieve in counseling; a clear picture of the anticipated result of therapy. When most people seek help, they hope that the counselor will make them better. However, this does not relieve counselees from personal involvement and responsibility in their counseling. Clients are not where they want to be and are at least somewhat motivated to tackle the counseling project. Outlining workable goals is not easy, but counselors who commit themselves to goal setting are likely to have a more successful counseling experience.

An adequate goal should answer six basic questions: (1) Who will do (2) what, (3) when, (4) to whom, (5) to what extent, and (6) under what conditions? Having an adequate goal requires, first, placing responsibility on the counselee; second, involving the counselor, if necessary, to assist in formulating and clarifying the goal; third, expecting counselors, if they continue treatment, to accept the goals as something they can work with; and fourth, determining a reasonable time frame for solving the problem.[1] Being so specific may seem cold and unfeeling to some people, yet those same people would not want their dentists to start working on the wrong tooth. Failing to answer these questions robs counseling of purpose.

Generating a sense of purpose is critical because individuals evaluate counseling by their sense of movement in the process and by their improved feelings. Goals provide purpose by:

1. setting direction: this reveals areas of counselee concern that need immediate attention; clarifies counselee expectations; establishes limitations of the counseling process; assures that the counselee's' specific needs are addressed;

2. giving counselors the opportunity to assess their own ability to meet counselees' expectations;

3. focusing the attention of the counselee cognitively, so counselors can encourage forward movement;

4. allowing for the appropriate selection of counseling techniques;

5. preparing for the process of outcome evaluation;

6. encouraging the counselee to take action as part of goal setting. Once the goal(s) are established the counselee may then have the requisite skills and/or knowledge to make the appropriate changes.[2]

Failing to furnish a purpose may start the counseling process on an endless struggle that lasts until one or both parties become discouraged and decide to quit.

IMPORTANCE OF GOAL SETTING

As noted in chapter 5, rapport becomes the first goal the counselor must have in developing the budding relationship. Yet rapport, though necessary, is not sufficient to maintain the counselee's belief in the value of counseling. If people sense that counseling is going nowhere, they begin to think about terminating therapy. Some success, however slight, early in the counseling process stimulates the desire for further progress.

FOUR ADVANTAGES OF GOAL SETTING

Goal setting has at least four advantages. First, setting goals focuses attention and action. New perspectives give counselees a vision toward which they can direct their energies. Counselees with goals are less likely to engage in aimless behavior. Second, setting goals mobilizes energy and effort. Clients who seem lethargic during problem exploration may come to life when faced with the question of spelling out alternate perspectives. Goal setting is not just a cognitive exercise; individuals begin moving toward goals in a variety of ways once they are set. Third, setting goals increases persistence. Not only are people with goals energized to do something, they also tend to work harder and longer. Clients with clear and realistic goals do not give up as easily as clients with vague goals or no goals at all. Fourth, setting goals leads naturally to a search for the means to accomplish them.[3] Once the goal is set and an assessment of the current condition made, the difference may seem far smaller than imagined. This can mobilize resources which have lain dormant to that point.

IMPORTANCE OF DIRECTION IN GOAL SETTING

In setting goals it is not only important to decide where you are going but also to establish markers which indicate whether what is desired is being accomplished. The former is direction, while the latter is the goal and/or subgoals.

Direction has several purposes in counseling. First, it provides a focus for the counseling process. Initially the counselee is mired in the confusing details of the problem. Remember the last time you were feeling overwhelmed by numerous tasks and felt paralyzed and unable to get any of them done? One way to get out of such a predicament is to write down what you have to do, then order the items starting with the most difficult. Tackling the more difficult first (if you are really discouraged, you might want to start with the easiest task just to get started) and getting it done affirms your direction and focus, which usually relieves the confusion and frustration. Counselees feel the same way. Giving them a focus by establishing a direction helps them determine what needs to be done first; that starts the counseling in a positive direction.

Direction also refocuses individuals on the present and future rather than the past. Since both the counselor and counselee desire a successful counseling outcome, they need to look to future results rather than causes. Directing the counselee's attention to the future lessens the emphasis on causes and digging for the root of the problem which, if it were known, would not change the present pain or future success of the counselee.[4] Even if the root cause were determined, the counselee would still need to make changes in the present to affect a satisfactory conclusion to counseling. The only exceptions to this axiom are people who just want to know the reasons for their problems and not the changes necessary to set their course in a successful direction.

Third, direction allows for planning. Stating specific and concrete descriptions of problems and goals is especially critical in the initial sessions because this is when the counselor formulates an understanding of the problem and makes therapeutic plans. Misunderstandings that result in inefficient plans at this juncture can take the therapy off course by miles.[5] In such cases the counselee has not or is not able to establish a suitable goal and therefore cannot move in the direction appropriate for taking the proper steps to improved behavior and feelings.

Direction implies not only planning but actions to be taken in reaching the goal. The counseling process is stymied until direction is established. Both counselor and counselee fail to see the way resources need to be channeled in order to realize a successful outcome. Selection of technique is critical here. With the focus and plan established, technique is easier to determine. For example, assertiveness training as a technique is ineffective until the counseling process determines a direction that calls for more assertiveness. Then the person who needs to gain assertiveness skills is focused and ready to move toward meeting other people in a more open and firm manner. In such cases the counseling process is organized and moving in a positive, future-oriented direction.

Maneuverability is another explicit result of having goals. Therapist-theorists at the Mental Research Institute in California maintain the necessity of maximizing therapist maneuverability while limiting counselee maneuverability. These investigators reason that counselees, like drowning swimmers, will resist therapeutic interventions, but limiting their maneuverability keeps the counselor in an advantageous position for planning therapy and intervening in problem situations.[6]

Counselors have more maneuverability and counselees are effectively limited by insisting that they be specific and concrete in establishing their goals for counseling. Suppose parents describe the change they expect in their son as a better attitude; such a vague goal permits them to consider that any change, even a small one, in the direction of improvement is not sufficient to meet their wishes. The effective counselor insists on a clear behavioral description of what constitutes an improved attitude. How would an improved attitude look to an outsider? It may mean better grades in school, but even that is not specific enough. Are D's acceptable over F's, or are the parents expecting all A's? Arriving at an acceptable grade as an indication of improved attitude, for example, is critical to moving the therapy beyond the goal-setting stage. Counselors must insist on specific and concrete goals.

HINDRANCES TO GOAL SETTING

The setting of goals will not always be accomplished easily. At least five hindrances will interfere with goal setting: difficulty in setting specific goals, a focus on feeling, resistance to responsibility, vague thinking, and lack of control.

DIFFICULTY IN SETTING SPECIFIC GOALS

Setting specific and concrete goals is hard work, and most people tend to avoid it in favor of finding an easier path to follow. Unfortunately, in counseling, this easier path often means formulating broad, vague, or general goals that do not allow for the efficient use of counseling time and the efforts of the counselee and counselor.[7] Difficulty in setting specific goals is just the first hindrance we must consider. While some obstacles are due to the counselor's style, theory, or lack of skills, other hindrances occur because the counselee fails to make specific goals.

Focus on Feeling

Some helpers, especially those who adopt a nondirective theory of counseling, focus on feelings rather than on the conditions producing or maintaining the client's problem. Considering feelings is important as long as this leads to a better understanding of the problem. A good use of feelings starts with naming the feeling and identifying what is generating it so that the problem situation can be changed.

Resistance to Responsibility

A few helpers may resist establishing concrete goals because they do not want to be held accountable for the results of the counseling. Such responsibility can weigh heavily on counselors, especially those who believe in a direct approach. Again, when the helper's theoretical approach includes vague goals (i.e., self-actualization) the counseling process is limited in direction from the very beginning. Some helpers think of client problems in vague ways. This allows the counselee to establish an unusable goal (or worse yet, no goal at all) to guide the counseling process.[8]

Vague Thinking

Counselees can also hamper goal setting by their tendency to think of problems in nonspecific ways.[9] De Shazer reports that only about one out of three counselees has the ability to think in specific and concrete terms about goals.[10] Perhaps the reason so few in counseling can think concretely is one reason they are in counseling; in contrast, those who think concretely and specifically can better formulate solutions for their own problems. Such unclear thinking may have been exacerbated by previous counseling experiences that lacked the focus of a specific goal.[11]

When describing goals, "uncertain, vague, or sweeping answers are common, since patients are like all of us: we are clearer about what we don't want than about what we do want."[12] Psychological pain may cloud a person's view of the future, and it is the clear-sighted helper who can assist the counselee in drawing a more focused picture of the desired goal. Persistence here is imperative.

LACK OF CONTROL

Another hindrance to goal setting is the tendency to think of problems as outside of people's control.[13] Putting the responsibility on another person is common where two or more people are involved. Establishing goals in such cases is difficult because the goal tends to be formulated in terms of what someone else must do. It is unlikely that someone other than the counselee will change, unless changes in the counselee provoke changes in the other person.[14] When someone else must change, the counselee is limited and subject to discouragement that may end the counseling process. Focusing on what the counselee can do to make life different is critical and will change the direction of therapy toward a productive end.

Goal setting must avoid labels and instead focus on behavior.[15] People often label themselves negatively. Jim, for example, might label his condition as depression and think of this as a common but unsolvable affliction. Jim's depression must be linked with what happens either in his thinking process or behavior and in the environment that supports the depressed mood. The helper must convert such labels into behaviors and thoughts in order to free the counselee to make useful changes.

Hindrances, then, are varied and difficult to manage. To overcome them we need good counselor skills. We must be persistent to describe the goal in workable, behavioral terms. We must abandon vague, although sophisticated, psychological terms and adopt specific and concrete language to move into the other person's world in such a way that change can occur. Even though responsibility for successful counseling needs to be shared with the counselee, counselors cannot ignore their part by failing to help people formulate concrete and workable goals.

CHARACTERISTICS OF GOALS

Goals generally fall into one of two categories: process and content. Process goals center on activities and/or procedures the counselor wants to accomplish as part of the therapy.

Content goals focus on what counselees seek as a result of counseling. Counselors can depend on having several process goals they will seek to complete as their part in guiding counseling. These include establishing rapport, developing a friendly and accepting climate, demonstrating empathy and positive regard, defining the problem, and obtaining the attempted solutions. Process goals are usually the same for everyone, whereas content goals change with each person.[16] Outcome goals are unique wishes which can include assertiveness, improved mood, and openness.

CONCRETE AND SPECIFIC

To be effective, goals must be concrete and specific, practical, positive, consistent, and difficult. Short-term counseling is based on the specificity of the goals, the active role of the counselor, and the expectations of a shorter therapy process necessitating that the counselee get to work more quickly.[17] In long-term counseling a vague goal poses less problem because there is ample time to work out what the counselee wants. In short-term counseling, with its limited time frame, it is critical to use every opportunity to define carefully the counselee's goals. Limited time prohibits our use of random approaches; we must address the pertinent issues as quickly as possible. "It is essential to focus on areas that will yield the highest dividends. Generally these deal with problems of immediate concern to the patient."[18]

By now it may seem redundant to say that goals must be specific and concrete. Yet even the most experienced counselors face the problem of letting people set vague or general goals, and thus sending the therapy drifting into an uncertain course. Ambiguous goals serve as sand traps keeping people from making the kinds of effective changes that would result in successful outcomes such as a happier, less troublesome, and more interesting life.[19]

However, occasions do arise when a vague goal is useful. People sometimes seek counseling because they are too rigid in their approach to solving problems.[20] The rigid counselee, who needs to exercise less control and learn to live with uncertainty, finds a vague goal, although painful, an appropriate part of treatment; but such a situation is the exception and not the rule.[21]

Esoteric counseling terms such as self-actualization, human potential, and existential vacuum also keep the counselor and counselee from setting the specific and concrete goals necessary to promote progress. "Pop" psychology has greatly added to the problem of esoteric language, and it challenges the counselor to spell out in clear and concrete language the definition of the problem and the description of the outcome. O'Hanlon and Wilk describe these esoteric terms as "empty"[22] and insist on verifiable descriptions of the process and what the counselee wants to happen as a result of counseling.[23]

PRACTICAL

Goals should not only be concrete and specific, they should also be practical. Only goals stated in terms of what the counselee will do differently are viable.[24] Viable goals with intrinsic reinforcement perpetuate themselves. Success encourages people to continue setting other goals and solving other problems. Failing will only convince people that they are not able to change, a conclusion resulting in a stall or possibly serious decline in counseling.[25] Co-creating an impossible goal for counseling jeopardizes a successful outcome right from the beginning. Avoid this pitfall by asking yourself whether the goal can be achieved under ordinary circumstances by normal people. Sensible goals propel people into achieving the goal.

Viable goals are positive and encouraging to the beleaguered person who, in a last ditch effort, has turned to counseling for assistance.[26] Goals must be advantageous for the counselee, and, though obvious, it is nonetheless essential that the advantage be seen in the light of the cost. The formula,

$$\text{Benefit of Goal} = \text{Gain}/\text{Cost}$$

can inform the counselee about the value of the goal. A lofty goal with great gain likely will cost more than a simpler goal. Cormier and Cormier have formulated several counseling leads to help the counselee discover the value of the goal:

1. In what ways is it worthwhile to pursue this goal?

2. What do you see as the benefits of this change?

3. Who would benefit from this change and how?

4. What are some positive consequences that may result from this change?[27]

POSITIVE

Not only should goals be advantageous to counselees, they need to be stated in positive language. This means we need to secure from counselees what they will be doing as a result of therapy rather than what they will not be doing. Most often people will report what they do not want to do, leaving blank any picture of the future that they might try to draw. Stating goals in positive language is important because knowing what is to be done rather than what is not to be done triggers within counselees the skills and knowledge appropriate for solving the problem.

CONSISTENT

Value congruency is another important facet of workable goals.[28] Here the sensitive counselor can assist counselees to understand their personal values and to formulate goals consistent with those personal values. People must also own the goal whether they formulate it themselves or create it with the counselor. This sense of ownership draws the counselee into working for the goal. Time limits are part of the counselee's owning the goal, because what is scheduled for anytime is likely to get no time.

WORKABLE

The level of difficulty can have a significant influence on how the counselee reacts to the goal. A workable goal draws the person into action. Harder goals generate better performance than easier ones. Goals that challenge the individual produce greater results than vague goals. The presence of hard goals and knowledge of results positively relates to increased performance.[29] People can, however, describe goals that are unbalanced in their difficulty level. Workable goals are critical in short-term counseling. To set the goals too high assures that the therapeutic process will fail, while setting the goals too low means counseling can end with a meaningless sense of victory. Useful goals are neither too high or too low but challenging.

Counselees who subscribe to unrealistically high goals are often perfectionistic and demanding of themselves. Some people who fear failure set unrealistically high goals so they can't be blamed for not reaching them.[30] In contrast, when counselees set unrealistically low goals out of a fear of failure, the attainment of such low objectives results in a hollow victory that fails to provide them with what they want. Asking counselees to rate the difficulty of the goal on a scale of 1 to 10 can help them understand the level of difficulty they are placing on the objective.

FORMULATION OF GOALS

People tend to move from the problem statement right into solutions without taking the time to establish goals. In fact, de Shazer found that very few people are prepared or able to set goals and, therefore, are hampered in addressing problems in a systematic way.[31] If we do not slow the headlong rush toward solution, the counselee is likely to either waste valuable time and resources at best or fail and give up at worst. Furthermore, without effective goals people are prone to make whimsical decisions that will lead them in the wrong direction.[32]

RESPECTING PEOPLE

Helping people to understand the significance of goal setting facilitates counseling. For some it is enough to explain the usefulness of goals. For others, analogies or examples can illustrate the need for goals. Pointing out the value of having a pattern when making a dress, for example, can sharpen people's understanding of what needs to happen in counseling.

In helping counselees establish working goals, counselors must not give the impression that counselees are unable to think for themselves. Mutuality in goal setting is important for motivation. By taking over we imply that people do not know how to help themselves.[33]

Formulating useful goals, then, is not a unilateral process. O'Hanlon and Weiner-Davis contend that acceptable behavior patterns vary so drastically that it is impossible for counselors to prescribe which goal people should address. Exceptions to this contention, of course, would include illegal behavior or goals that are inconsistent with the counselor's value system or ability to counsel. Generally, counselees know better than counselors what they want to accomplish in counseling. Helping people express their wishes is the helper's responsibility.[34]

Goals emerge from people's wishes and dreams. The difference between wishes and reality produces the pain that brings them into counseling. Sometimes those dreams are vague and need clarification. Establishing goals brings the needed clarity so people progress with greater ease either on their own or with help. Because troubled people have problems formulating reachable goals, it is essential that the counselor guide the therapeutic conversation toward the establishment of goals counselors can reach themselves.

O'Hanlon and Weiner-Davis classify therapeutic conversation into "goal-oriented," "problem-oriented," and "yet-to-be-determined" categories.[35] Goal-oriented talk reveals behavior directly related to the therapeutic goal. Negative talk about events in life describes problem-oriented messages. When conversation fits neither category it is identified as yet-to-be-determined material. Of course the former and later categories should dominate the therapeutic hour.

CONCEIVING THE GOAL

Since counselees often do not know what they would like to accomplish in counseling, the counselor might ask, "If given three wishes, what would you wish?" Another approach is to ask what would happen if the counselee was free of the problem. Such an inquiry may be worded: "Does this problem happen all of the time?" Usually the person will say no, after which the counselor can ask, "What's life like when the problem is gone? Who is involved? How are the behaviors different? When does this happen?" These and similar questions help focus attention on a future without the problem.

Another approach asks people what it would be like for them if a miracle happened overnight and the problem were solved in the morning. Such procedures encourage people to think about more acceptable life patterns. Counselees usually focus on the problem and on the past, where nothing can be resolved. Focusing on the future turns the therapeutic process around and starts counselees on the road to finding ways to reach their goals.

Another avenue of approach is to ask the following questions early in the first interview:

1. What have you noticed that is different about your situation? (Clients often notice between the call for an appointment for therapy and the first session that things already seem different.)

2. Are these changes in the problem area?

3. Are these the kinds of changes you would like to continue to have happen?

Two-thirds of the counselees who were asked these questions at the Youth Service Bureau in Woodstock, Illinois, answered that changes had occurred in the problem situation and that they wanted them to continue happening in the future.

Prayer by the counselor and the counselee is also an important aspect of the solution. Effective prayer, however, is carefully aimed at what will make a significant difference. Here the Christian counselor can seek to establish specific prayer goals with counselees. Prayer commits counselees to being a part of the solution. One danger about prayer is that counselees may think their counselors are suggesting some kind of "spiritual magic" that will resolve the problem without the counselees' involvement.[36]

All is not lost, however, if people can only formulate general goals. Nonspecific goals, which are better than no goals at all, serve as a bridge to more specific objectives. Making goals more specific is a critical part of the counseling process and thrives only on what is clear to the counselee and counselor.[37] Converting a vague goal into a specific one is a perplexing problem facing most counselors. To facilitate this process, suggest a generic task that uses the person's language to tell him or her what to do before the next session. "For example, if a client wants 'more peace of mind,' suggest, 'Keep track of what you are doing this week that gives you more peace of mind.'"[38]

If people find it difficult to express the goal in concrete and observable terms, the counselor can ask what a companion, partner, or relative will notice that indicates real change. Getting people to view their problems through the eyes of other people can break the subjectivity and myopia that keep them from seeing what they want.[39] Try, also, teaching people how to form efficient goals by giving them instructions and examples to follow.[40] It sometimes helps to break the problem down into understandable parts: resources, people, skills, behaviors, feelings, thoughts, time needed—the elements necessary to accomplish the goal. Such a breakdown also reveals the obstacles that must be faced in order to reach the goal.

Strategies for working with people who will not or cannot set goals include: (1) the counselor's setting goals and the counselee reviewing them, (2) the counselor's asking for a small, even trivial, goal to start the goal-setting process,[41] and (3) the counselor's declaring a state of helplessness and forcing the counselee into a position of responsibility.[42]

Finally, when the counselor has exhausted the usual efforts to get a person to be specific about the goal of counseling, it might be best to accept vagueness as the problem and proceed from there.[43] Our first task in such situations is to start people thinking about life in concrete ways. For example, we might ask them to describe their family, and then help them stay with concrete terms by pointing out when they are specific and when they are vague. Describing for counselees what constitutes admissible evidence in a court of law may help them conceptualize more concretely. Whichever technique the counselor chooses, the goal of counseling at this point is to ameliorate counselee vagueness.

The elements people include in their goal statements produce other problems hindering the conceptualization of the goal. For example, some counselees want another person to change, a task obviously dependent on whether that person wants to change and is willing to come into the counseling process. Counselees must recognize that the people most likely to change are the ones in the counseling process. Changes in people not in counseling cannot be guaranteed.

Another hindrance to setting useful goals is the utopian expectations some people have. Counselors can try to point out the unreasonableness of such goals, or they can go even higher in their stated aspirations for the counselee. Raising the goal shows how others might evaluate the unreasonably high goals. Going beyond the lofty goal also encourages them to take control and reduce the goal to a more reasonable level.[44] When set too low, goals can be built into a larger context. This can help facilitate a broader view of the problem situation. For example, Weeks and L'Abate report helping a man get back into the work force after a simple schizophrenic episode by combining his reluctance to get a job (the real goal) with his determination to write a book.[45] The counselor suggested that he write about job-hunting techniques. In order to research his book the counselee went on interviews for several jobs, one of which he accepted for himself.

The following description by Egan summarizes the qualities of effective goals: ownership, appeal, options, reduction of crisis and pain, detailed scenarios, challenge, management of distinctives, contracts, and action strategies.

- Energy is released when the counselee owns the goal. Responsibility is directly on the one who owns the goal.

- Attractiveness makes the commitment and execution of the goal more likely.

- Avoid having your counselees feel forced into a choice by helping them to develop more than one alternative to choose from.

- If the goal directly reduces pain or ameliorates a crisis the counselee is more likely to stay with the commitment.

- Positive images and descriptive detail in the alternative of choice helps to draw energy and commitment from the counselee.

- When partial success is coupled with a challenging alternative, the counselee is more likely to put forth the effort to accomplish the goal.

- Finding ways for the counselee to meet and overcome obstacles enhances the commitment process.

- A personal commitment to one's self can assist the counselee in staying with the goal-oriented changes when the going gets tough.

- Specific actions which, when taken, will get the counselee started in the accomplishment of the desired goal can begin in the consulting room before the counselee leaves.[46]

Having people state the mutually-agreed-upon goal in their own words assures that they understand what is to happen between sessions. Such a rehearsal gives the counselor the opportunity to clarify and reinforce the goal behavior.[47]

IMPLEMENTATION OF GOALS

With a workable goal in place, the counselor must turn to guiding the client toward implementation or achievement of the goal. The first phase is commitment to change. This must be related to the value the counselee places on the results of the new behavior: "How would life be different if this goal were accomplished? What satisfactions would accomplishing this goal have for me? To what degree would it take care of the concerns I am feeling right now? To what degree would it be an implementation of values I hold dear?" On the other hand, the counselee might ask, "What would life be like if this goal were not to be accomplished? Would it mean that my present concerns would not be substantially managed?"[48]

Most behavior is contingent on how the results of the behavior are perceived. Higher rewards, whether internal or external, are positively correlated with goal acceptance. External rewards are those reinforcers that come from outside the person and may include money, prestige, or power. Internal rewards, coming from within the counselee, produce feelings of accomplishment, self-referred words of praise, satisfaction of a job well done. Internal reinforcement is preferred over external reinforcement because it represents a learning that is independent of other people in the environment. It also increases the likelihood the counselee will continue in the newly established behavioral pattern without the influence of the counselor.

Pressure from supervisors, experimenters, and authorities in general will likely increase goal performance. This suggests that the counselor can maximize the effect of the goal by maintaining contact with the individual to see how goal attainment is progressing. Phone calls between sessions tell the person that the counselor remembers what goal was established and that counselor interest goes beyond the therapeutic hour.

Another phase of implementation involves having the counselee make some small change as preparation for other changes. Success is more likely if the goal of change is reasonably small and clearly stated.[49] Asking a person for a change, any change that makes sense, right from the first session moves individuals into the habit of making changes. In other words, change begets change. Asking the counselee to keep a record of the symptom provides just such a change because writing down the time, place, and circumstances of the symptom means the counselee is not experiencing the symptom in the same context as before; it introduces a change in the problem situation.

If all things are equal people usually choose a goal when they have high rather than low expectations of reaching it. In this phase not only do people need to view the goal as attainable, but they must also believe they can accomplish what is necessary to reach the goal.[50]

Another important phase in goal achievement is taking inventory of the resources available. Potential resources include feelings, thoughts and belief systems, people, situations, information, and skills. Evaluation and inclusion of existing resources increases the likelihood of successfully achieving the identified goal.

Sometimes resources are redistributed from old patterns of behavior to new and potentially threatening routines. Paul's injunctions in Ephesians illustrate the concept of redistribution:

You were taught, with regard to your former way of life, to put off your old self, which being corrupted by its deceitful desires; to be made new in the attitude of your minds; and to put on the new self, created to be like God in true righteousness and holiness (4:22–24).

The putting off of the old necessitates the redistribution of resources to the new self and its ways. Changing from one goal or way of behavior to another means shifting personal strengths, abilities, and time.[51] Part of redistributing resources involves weighing the value of one goal against how its accomplishment detracts from another more desirable end.[52] Inventorying and redistributing resources requires careful thought about the people included in the change process. Generally, success is more likely when the therapeutic outcome is not dependent on other individuals because it is often difficult to get others involved. Involving other people may involve the formation of yet another goal.[53]

Not only must people inventory resources, they must also plan for overcoming obstacles.[54] Noting and preparing to deal with obstacles is imperative if the counselee is to accomplish the goal. Setting goals can reveal possible obstacles which, when addressed early in the problem solving process, need not doom the project to failure.

During the sequencing phase, breaking a larger goal into smaller pieces is a concrete step which helps counselees proceed toward mastery of the objective. More basic subgoals should be accomplished before the counselee goes on to a new subgoal. New behaviors should be practiced on a daily basis. When the counselee fails to accomplish small daily changes, the first subgoal needs to be reconsidered and tailored to make it accomplishable. Sequencing can also include evaluating the importance of the goal in its relationship to other goals. This puts it into a frame where people can decide if they can proceed with commensurate action and not destroy another highly valued goal.

Goals should serve as guides for behavior, but not as rigid rules keeping people from exercising good sense in reformulating any goal that does not meet with their wishes. Counselors must be sensitive to allow for modifications of how people coordinate the goal with its many components. Counselor discontent with progress may, however, communicate criticism to the counselee, so comments should be framed in as positive a light as possible. Since people usually start counseling with a sense of defeat, it is important that they have every opportunity to feel successful about what they are doing.

COUNSELING CAN END HERE

Can establishing a goal help people achieve, without further counseling, what they want for their lives? Certainly! Consider how frequently you have been troubled but unable to formulate what you wanted. How much easier it was when you could imagine a life without the complaint. In fact, once the goal is set a person may then know what skills and resources are necessary to accomplish it. A concrete goal may unleash unused abilities which have developed in non-problem situations, but have never been applied to the problem. Goal formulation takes people's eyes off of the pain and the past and puts them on a future without the pain. Just picturing the desired end draws a person in the direction of problem solution. So counseling can end here, because people are usually problem solvers and when they get a clear idea of what to do, they move with renewed energy and rechanneled skills.

FINALLY

This chapter has focused our attention on the importance of setting goals. We have considered several aspects of establishing a concrete, specific, and workable goal. These aspects have included the importance of goal setting, hindrances people face in setting goals, characteristics of goals, formulation, and finally, implementation of goals. Most individuals will not automatically express their problems in goal-related language, and counselors frequently do not help people establish useful therapeutic goals. Even though goal setting is difficult, effective counselors must commit themselves to helping their counselees set, shape, and put into operation goals that will lead them out of their problems.

NOTES

1. Gerald Weeks and Luciano L'Abate, *Paradoxical Psychotherapy: Theory and practice with individuals, couples, and families* (New York: Bruner/Mazel, 1982), 78.

2. William Cormier and L. Sherilyn Cormier, *Interviewing Strategies for Helpers: Fundamental skills and cognitive behavioral interventions* (Pacific Grove, Calif.: Brooks/Cole, 1991), 217–18.

3. E. A. Locke and G. P. Latham, *Goal Setting: A motivational technique that works* (Englewood Cliffs, N. J.: Prentice-Hall, 1984).

4. W. Backus, *Telling the Truth to Troubled People* (Minneapolis: Bethany House, 1985), 37.

5. R. Fisch, J. H. Weakland, and L. Segal, *The Tactics of Change: Doing brief therapy* (San Francisco: Jossey-Bass, 1982), 33–34.

6. Fisch, Weakland, and Segal, *Tactics of Change*, 21–24.

7. Wayne Dyer, "A Goal-Setting Checklist for Counselors," *Personnel and Guidance Journal* 55, no. 8 (1977), 470.

8. Weeks and L'Abate, *Paradoxical Psychotherapy*, 78–79.

9. Harold Hackney, "Goal-Setting: Maximizing the reinforcing effects of progress," *The School Counselor* (January 1973), 176–77.

10. Steve de Shazer, *Keys to Solution in Brief Therapy* (New York: Norton, 1985), 9.

11. Weeks and L'Abate, *Paradoxical Psychotherapy*, 78–79.

12. Fisch, Weakland, and Segal, *Tactics of Change*, 79.

13. Hackney, "Goal-Setting," 176–177.

14. Bill O'Hanlon and James Wilk, *Shifting Contexts: The generation of effective psychotherapy* (New York: Guilford, 1987), 73.

15. Hackney, "Goal-Setting: Maximizing the reinforcing effects of progress," *The School Counselor* (January 1973), 176–77.

16. E. Locke et al., "Goal Setting and Task Performance, 1969–1980," *Psychological Bulletin* 90, no. 1 (1981), 125–52.

17. S. Garfield, *The Practice of Brief Psychotherapy* (Elmsford, N. Y.: Pergamon, 1989), 12.

18. Lewis Wolberg, *Handbook of Short-term Psychotherapy* (New York: Thieme-Stratton, 1980), 157.

19. See Paul Watzlawick and James Weakland, eds., *The Interactional View: Studies at the Mental Research Institute, Palo Alto (1965–1974)* (New York: Norton, 1977), 316–17; and A. Nezu, C. Nezu and M. Perri, *Problem-Solving Therapy for Depression: Theory, research and clinical guidelines* (New York: John Wiley & Sons, 1981), 78.

20. M. F. Weiner, *Practical Psychotherapy* (New York: Bruner/Mazel, 1986), 99, 111.

21. Jay Haley, *Problem-Solving Therapy: New strategies for effective family therapy* (San Francisco: Jossey-Bass, 1976), 41.

22. See O'Hanlon and Wilk, *Shifting Contexts*, 74–82; and Carl Thoresen and Jane Anton, "Intensive Counseling," *Focus on Guidance* 6, no. 2 (October 1973), 4.

23. See Hackney, "Goal-Setting," 177–78; and Thoresen and Anton, "Intensive Counseling," 4.

24. Gerard Egan, *The Skilled Helper: A systematic approach to effective helping*, 4th ed. (Pacific Grove, Calif.: Brooks/Cole, 1990), 299–302, 306.

25. Dyer, "A Goal-Setting Checklist," 470–71.

26. Egan, *The Skilled Helper*, 306.

27. Cormier and Cormier, *Interviewing Strategies*, 224.

28. See Egan, *Skilled Helper*, 306; and Backus, *Telling the Truth*, 40.

29. Locke, et al., "Goal Setting," 127–34.

30. D. N. Dixon and J. A. Glover, *Counseling: A problem-solving approach* (New York: Wiley, 1984), 133.

31. Steve de Shazer, *Keys to Solutions in Brief Therapy* (New York: Norton, 1985), 9.

32. See Egan, *The Skilled Helper*, 290.

33. Dyer, "A Goal-Setting Checklist," 470.

34. Wlliam O'Hanlon and M. Weiner-Davis, *In Search of Solutions: A new direction in psychotherapy* (New York: Norton, 1989), 43–44.

35. O'Hanlon and Weiner-Davis, *In Search of Solutions*, 82–83, 103, 106, 166–167.

36. Backus, *Telling the Truth*, 36.

37. See Hackney, "Goal-Setting," 179.

38. O'Hanlon and Weiner-Davis, *In Search of Solutions*, 138.

39. de Shazer, *Keys to Solutions*, 5.

40. Watzlawick and Weakland, *The Interactional View*, 286.

41. D. Gordon and M. Meyers-Anderson, *Phoenix: Therapeutic patterns of Milton H. Erickson* (Cupertino, Calif.: Meta Publications, 1981), 121.

42. Paul Watzlawick, J. Beavin, and Don Jackson, *Pragmatics of Human Communication: A study of interactional patterns, pathologies, and paradoxes* (New York: Norton, 1967), 67–70.

43. Fisch, Weakland, and Segal, *Tactics of Change*, 88.

44. Watzlawick and Weakland, *The Interactional View*, 286.

45. Weeks and L'Abate, *Paradoxical Psychotherapy*, 81.

46. Egan, *Skilled Helper*, 313–20.

47. Dyer, "A Goal-Setting Checklist," 471.

48. Egan, *The Skilled Helper*, 307.

49. Watzlawick and Weakland, *The Interactional View*, 282.

50. Albert Bandura, "Self-efficacy: Toward a unifying theory of behavioral change," *Psychological review* 84, no. 2 (1977), 193ff. See chapter 4 for a discussion of expectancy of success and efficacy expectancy.

51. Egan, *Skilled Helper*, 311–12.

52. Locke, et al., "Goal Setting," 127.

53. Nezu, Nezu and Perri, *Problem-Solving Therapy for Depression*, 38.

54. C. Hughes, *Goal Setting: Key to individual and organizational effectiveness* (American Management Association, 1965), 113–15.

PART THREE

The Change

Chapter Nine

Facilitating Change: Liberating the Client

T HIS CHAPTER LOOKS FORWARD to the intervention phase of counseling. It also looks back at the eight preceding chapters where we have considered the first four steps of short-term counseling that can lead to life-altering and problem-relieving change(s). As we have noted, these steps are: developing a therapeutic relationship by cultivating rapport, describing the problem as solvable, discovering what attempts have been made to solve the problem, and establishing an achievable goal. Actually, these four steps are interventions. Starting with a review of how each of these four steps is an intervention, this chapter also considers the principles of intervention.

RAPPORT

Reflective listening is the cornerstone of developing any relationship, social or therapeutic. It is a rare experience, especially for those who are hurting, to find someone who really listens. Good listening carries several benefits. It lets the person talking know he or she is accepted, an element critical to healing. Acceptance does not mean we approve of everything the other person has done, but it does convey the warmth so necessary in making people feel welcomed and loved.

Good listening also builds empathy, creating the kind of atmosphere conducive to getting at, changing, and solving problems. People need permission to change, and that kind of permission requires unconditional acceptance and positive regard. Only then are people set free to make the alterations necessary to bring renewed health. Why is this true?

As long as the counselor struggles to get people to change, they resist because of their need to maintain their own autonomy. Unconditional acceptance allows them to keep their problems, if they wish, but also frees them to evaluate and make changes. Unconditional acceptance was the key to change in Carl Rogers's person-centered counseling and is the essence of the rapport building stage of short-term counseling. Our human understanding of unconditional acceptance mirrors the unconditional love (*agape*) that God has for His people and that He asks us to show to others. Because of God's unconditional love we can choose to make the changes necessary in our lives to bring us closer to Him and to healthier living.

Listening also increases the counselee's level of creativity necessary to solve problems. How often have you found that nothing more than effective listening has helped stimulate new ideas? One person can generate volumes of creative ideas, *if* judgment of the ideas is suspended until after the creative session. Unconditional acceptance promotes the kind of atmosphere that encourages the production of good ideas, any one of which may be the solution to the problem.

Effective listening means not only hearing and understanding what was said, but also letting the other person know what you have heard. This provides people with a kind of verbal mirror, allowing them to hear what they are saying and to make judgments about their own thinking. In an atmosphere of safety and positive regard, people do not need to defend themselves and are, therefore, more open to considering matters objectively. Objectivity can generate alternate ways of seeing and feeling about situations and problems.

Solomon recognized the wisdom of listening, "He who answers before listening—that is his folly and his shame" (Prov. 18:13). Beware of answering before listening, of daydreaming and creating answers while another person is talking. Responses formulated this way demonstrate that you are only interested in getting to your response, not in listening to what the other person has said. Effective listening respects the other person and his or her thoughts, feelings, expressions—and words.

PROBLEM DEFINITIONS

Usually people do not know how to think about their problems, but as they talk they are able to clarify what is hurting them. Effective listening helps people clarify what is happening in their lives that is painful. Problem definition, step two of our short-term model, is also an intervention. Getting people to describe specifically what is bothering them often leads them to concrete answers overlooked before the therapeutic encounter. The value of specific descriptions of problems, like listening, brings what was vague yet hurtful into focus so clearly that the answer may become obvious.

DISCOVERING EXISTING SOLUTIONS

Utilizing existing solutions is a benefit of the third step of short-term counseling, determining attempted solutions. Asking for these solutions also provides an intervention that can yield remarkable results. Often people who come for help have forgotten what has worked in the past. It could be that the symptoms of the new problem are different enough that the person fails to recognize the connection between what was a problem, what solved it, and the current problem. Identifying these solutions also allows for the discovery of strengths buried in the dust created by failure. The process of identifying existing solutions and helping people realize their strengths invokes a very powerful intervention—changing attitudes that have kept people locked in misery and despair.

STATING A GOAL

Establishing a concrete and workable goal, the fourth step in short-term counseling, is another intervention yielding remarkable results. Too often people have no realization of what they want to accomplish as the result of counseling. This fogginess keeps them from setting a course that would get them much closer to where they want to be. Clearly defining the target not only sets the direction, it also releases the energy and creativity necessary to get there. Generally, when people have goals they start moving toward those goals by conscious and unconscious effort. For example, having a person make a "wish list" and then put it away so it can be examined in a few weeks can result in changes which, when they are recognized, so encourage the person that he or she continues to make other changes and approximates the level of health necessary for happiness.

PRINCIPLES OF INTERVENTION

Intervention begins with the initial interview. To intervene is inevitable; therefore, every move demands careful consideration. Some principles of intervening will guide the counselor in the efficient use of counseling time.

READINESS

The first involves timing. Research in education has demonstrated that children learn when they are ready. Readiness is also a factor in making an effective intervention. Part of preparing the person is providing a positive atmosphere that encourages change.[1] Beyond atmosphere is the sense of urgency that people feel when they recognize a discrepancy between where they are and the goal established in counseling. Readiness depends on the safety of the situation allowing for free examination of the problem situation, the counselor's own judgments about what is seen and felt, and ownership of the goal(s) established as a function of counseling.

Fit

A second principle for a successful intervention is fit. Do the interventions make sense to people when seen from their perspectives? If not, there is a poor fit and the intervention is likely to fail. In order to make a fit the counselor must understand the person's view of self, the world, and God. For example, asking parents to do something completely opposed to their view of parenting is certainly not likely to succeed. This failure comes not because the intervention is bad, but because it does not make sense to the person.

Adaptation

Allowing for the adaptation of the intervention is another important principle of successfully intervening. People tend to personalize suggestions. When a counselor gives a suggestion, an individual will usually make some modification, even a small one, that does not necessarily change the intervention substantially but does personalize it. Making a vague assignment permits such adaptation. For example, if you want the person to exercise physically, but you want to allow for adaptation, recommend three or four possibilities from which he or she can choose. The person may then select an entirely different exercise, yet one acceptable to you. Choosing an odd or difficult exercise invites them to modify the suggestion by picking an exercise they would *rather* do. Either way the effect is the same.

Interruption

With the problem defined as a behavior, an intervention which is likely to be successful interrupts the behavioral pattern of the problem. To illustrate, recall the case of the man (in chapter 6) who, after leaving the house, would return to make certain that he had closed the windows and turned off the stove. I told him to check all he wanted, but when he entered the house the second time, he was to remove his shoes *and* socks before going through his checking routine. He stopped checking because each time he approached the door to leave he would wonder whether he had checked everything so he would not have to return and remove his shoes and socks. My intervention simply added a new, inconvenient, and disagreeable behavior. Pattern interruption is a powerful intervention, especially when the problem is voluntary behavior. Involuntary problems are best treated with symptom prescription.

PARADOX

Closely related to personalizing an intervention is the consideration of the obstinacy of human will. People tend to do the opposite of what they are told to do. This is more evident in some people than in others, but is evident frequently enough for consideration as a principle for successful intervening. Generally most interventions that account for obstinacy fall under the rubric of paradoxical counseling.Briefly, paradoxical counsel involves prescribing the symptom—actually telling a counselee to maintain or increase the symptom. The technique requires careful thought and planning and is used only when the counselor is willing to have the person actually carry out the assignment.[2]

REFRAMING

Reframing powerfully influences the counselee because it interferes with how the problem has been classified. When a behavior, feeling, or thought legitimately belongs to more than one category or classification, it allows for a reframe. For example, the man who was labeled "fishy" by his wife was reframed as "flexible." Once she saw him in an alternate frame, she was unable to return completely to the old one, a change which significantly influenced their relationship.

Reframing and paradox are covered in detail in chapters 10 and 11.

NOTES

1. Moshe Talmon, *Single-Session Therapy: Maximizing the effect of the first (and often only) therapeutic encounter* (San Francisco: Jossey-Bass, 1990), 36–37.

2. Obviously, suicide and homicide are examples of when symptom prescription is inappropriate.

Chapter Ten

Reframing

Robert Fulghum whimsically entitled his book *All I Really Need to Know I Learned in Kindergarten*, a simple but jarring reframe of the complexities of life. The rules he distills from his kindergarten experience include, in part:

1. Share everything.
2. Play fair.
3. Don't hit people.
4. Put things back where you found them.
5. Clean up your own mess.
6. Don't take things that aren't yours.
7. Say you're sorry when you hurt somebody.
8. Wash your hands before you eat.
9. Flush.

10. Warm cookies and cold milk are good for you.

11. Live a balanced life.

12. Take a nap every afternoon.

13. When you go out into the world, watch out for traffic, hold hands, and stick together.

14. Be aware of wonder.

15. All things die.

16. Look around you.[1]

When we apply these simple rules to adult situations, they have the curious effect of making life seem simple and do-able. How many fights would be avoided if we played fair and did not hit? Tranquility would rule the household where people said they were sorry when they hurt others or where people cleaned up after themselves. These kindergarten rules obviously make sense, but we too rarely remember or practice them. Fulghum's book powers its way into our minds by maneuvering us into viewing our adult behavior through the eyes of a kindergartner. He effectively shifts the frame by which we judge things from adult justifications to the simple but indisputable simplicity of a child.

WHAT IS REAL?

What allows Fulghum to make this kind of cognitive shift? Is reality so fluid that it permits such thought-exploding reframes? Chapter 3 provides a discussion of how human beings place meaning on stimuli or the events surrounding them. Here we limit ourselves to framing, the coalescing of stimuli into meaningful patterns that allow people to understand the data they receive through the five senses. Frames are not reality, and therefore are subject to change that may significantly affect how life is managed.

On reflection it becomes obvious that anything is real only to the extent that it conforms to a definition of reality—and those definitions are legion. To employ a useful oversimplification: real is what a sufficiently large number of people have agreed to call real—except that this fact is usually forgotten; the agreed-upon definition is reified (that is made into a "thing" in its own right) and is eventually experienced as that objective reality "out there" which apparently only a madman can fail to see.[2]

Let me assure you that we are not promoting the idea that there is no reality or evidence or actuality, but only that what we experience subjectively is real to us in a way that is different from the reality other people experience. Simply put, reality is more personal, and actuality is factual and verifiable by other people. Counselees' complaints include actual evidence plus interpretations of that evidence. Evidence, or the facts of the problem situation, consisting of behaviors, words, incidences, etc., do not change; but the interpretations or frames, the subject matter of counseling, are amenable to change.[3]

These interpretations consist of divisions that we arbitrarily place on the data. For example, our perception of time consists of the divisions of night, day, hours, minutes, and seconds. We measure things by dividing the length, breadth, and height into inches, feet, and yards, or, to illustrate the changeableness of an interpretation, we can use the metric system to measure the same thing. Human understanding rests on making divisions, separating "things" into different categories without which we would be hopelessly lost in a world of sameness. Not only do people interpret sensory data by dividing them into various categories, but they also join together elements to make a new understanding. Creativity joins disparate elements to form new ideas. Putting things together, which is just as important as dividing things into categories, provides for better understanding. In counseling we seek to learn how people divide and join the evidence, and make changes in those divisions and joinings to promote a healthier outlook.[4]

How we understand data or evidence also depends on our language. All language is symbolic and abstract,[5] and illustrates the fluidity of human interpretations that can lead people into problems or into success, depending on how they abstract facts. Hayakawa illustrates this abstraction process by talking about Bessie.

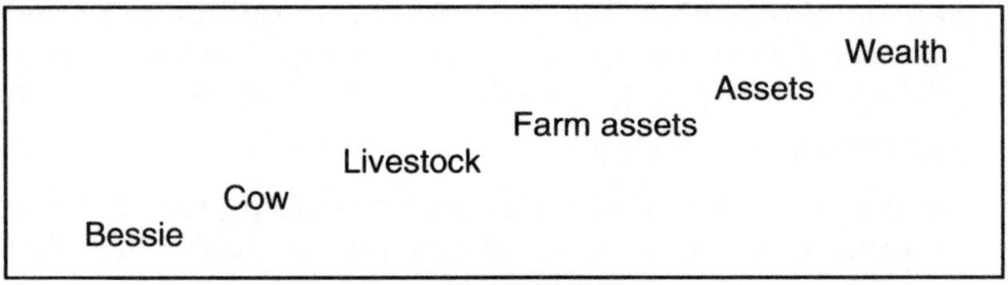

Abstraction Process
Figure 10–1

All of the labels for Bessie, shown in figure 10–1, are true, but some are more useful than others for certain purposes. For example, the economics professor uses the asset or wealth abstraction to illustrate a point regarding managing money, whereas the auctioneer refers to livestock, and the father to his daughter, Bessie, which personalizes the animal. Abstractions permeate our language system and may just as likely confuse as help our understanding.[6]

THEOLOGY DIVIDES AND JOINS

Since the Bible is the Word of God, it is factual and must be treated as evidence. When we study the Bible, we are looking at hard data, and because the Bible is so large, we divide it into books, chapters, and verses for ease of referencing and clarity of understanding. By using interpretative tools, scholars take the evidence of Scripture, and divide and join that evidence into larger patterns to formulate doctrine and subsequent theological systems. The reason so many different theologies exist directly relates to how the words are divided and the concepts joined. All interpretation, whether of Scripture or daily conversation, is an exacting process. Obstacles wait to destroy effective communication like rocks against a floundering ship. Great care and skill must be employed to successfully avoid a disastrous conclusion. Fortunately, the Bible is not subject only to private interpretation, for we can rest in the deliberations of many people who work diligently to give us a true and accurate understanding of the Scriptures and God.

Nature of Reframing

Reframing changes the meaning or understanding placed on objective actuality by an individual. Such changes are possible because there is no one psychological explanation or theory to which all other interpretations must bow. Reality as defined in a psychiatric sense, for example, is not the "thing" itself but only a term or label substituted for the actual "thing." Labels or diagnoses derived from theory are above things they describe in the sense that they are not the same but give meaning or understanding to actual things. Making a distinction between subjective reality and objective actuality can assist us in keeping these two categories exclusive.[7]

"It [reframing] breaks the illusionary frame inherent in any world image, and thereby reveals that what appeared unchangeable can indeed be changed and that there exist superordinate alternatives."[8] Dolan uses picture frames to illustrate reframing.[9] A green frame brings out even the smallest amount of green in a picture, but changing the frame to blue de-emphasizes green and enhances blue. Reframing does not change the facts of a situation, but it does bring out other aspects making a significant difference in how people perceive and behave. That is the goal of reframing and counseling.

We are limited by how we view things, and this is controlled in a large part by the culture in which we are reared. Culture means not only the macroculture of our society but also the microculture of the family into which we were born. When either of these cultures places an unsolvable frame on a problem, reframing is an appropriate, and likely successful, way of getting people to see there are ways of changing what seems unchangeable.

Reframing works directly on the interpretations or attributions placed on the facts. Attributions and interpretations permitting people to understand the data they receive through the five senses are subject to cultural influences and do not necessarily represent truth. Therefore, people are free to change in ways that are healthier. We must remember, however, that once an interpretation is made it may be very difficult to change.

William O'Hanlon cites the following as common attributions that can cause communicational and psychological problems.

1) Attributions. This involves assigning some quality, characteristics or relationships to data. Varieties include:

a) Causal attributions—claims of cause or effect (e.g., "She made me mad," or "I can't because of my background.")

b) Attributions of intentions, motivations, purpose and function—claims of reasons "behind" actions and experience (e.g., "He does that just to bug me," or "I must want to punish myself.")

c) Attributions of personality traits (characterization) — claims of internal psychological or emotional qualities to people (e.g., "He is lazy," or "I think I'm insane.")

d) Attributions of internal experience to others—often called "mind-reading"—claiming knowledge of someone else's feelings, thoughts or experience (e.g., "He's angry," or "I know you're sitting there judging me.")

2) Classifying and grouping. This involves categorizing, joining, and distinguishing the data:

a) Classification—assigning an element to a class of elements (e.g., "He's an American," or "Positive connotation is one type of reframing.")

b) Naming—assigning a label to an experience or element (e.g., "That's jazz," or "My name is Bill.")

c) Generalization—when one or some elements are said to be a larger group or the whole class of elements (e.g., "She's always late," or "If I've told you once, I've told you a million times.")

d) Characterizing adjectives—assigning some quality to some experience (e.g., "That was a bright idea," or "That was an inefficient way of doing that.")

e) Equivalences—one experience is said to be identical to another (e.g., "Love is never having to say you're sorry," or "Silence is an admission of guilt.")

f) Linking—two or more elements are said to be associated (e.g., "Those dishes go together," or "This is just like my last breakdown.")

g) Splitting—drawing boundaries and sequences (e.g., "He hit me first," or "It's the first day of spring.")

3) Evaluations—assigning a value or judgment on the worth or importance of something or someone (e.g., "That's not important right now," or "It was a valuable experience for me.")

4) Conclusions (or implications of significance)—drawing a conclusion about the meaning or implication of an experience (e.g., "His presence in therapy indicates that he is committed to the marriage.")

a) Predictions—claiming knowledge of the future (e.g., "He'll never amount to anything," or "She's going to experience that grief sooner or later.")

5) Metaphor. These are image or phrases used to describe or communicate experience in a non-literal way.

a) Analogies—when one thing is likened to another (e.g., "Your son is really like a husband," or "I feel like I'm in a deep, dark hole.")

b) Metaphorical frames—when an image is implicit in a description (e.g., "Mind was racing a mile a minute. I was a million miles away," shows the "thoughts as travelers" frame.)

c) Metaphor—when a story (characterized by description of action and a beginning, middle, and end) is told (e.g., "Once a man wanted to find out whether computers could think like humans. So he gathered all the best computer programmers and equipment around him and set them to the task of answering the questions. When preparations were complete, he typed in the questions: DO YOU COMPUTE THAT YOU CAN THINK LIKE A HUMAN BEING? After some time, the printer began typing, THAT REMINDS ME OF A STORY. . . ."[10]

Reframing leads to insight, a change of classification that is memorable and potentially life changing. Strange, humorous, and/or odd reframes may stick better than overused or ordinary ones. Gibson reframed a man, who was taking major responsibility for child care and homemaking but who felt unappreciated, as "Gary Poppins."[11]

A common experience illustrates the powerful effect of framing. When approached by a person who talks about some issue of interest to me, I feel an emotional openness and vulnerability. The awareness that he is a salesman, however, triggers within me a change of frame and an immediate emotional closure. He has something to gain from what he is saying—"Beware," I say to myself, and I am sure he senses this closure, too. Perhaps you have heard someone read a list of behaviors that includes insurrection, imprisonment, and rioting only to discover the person described is the apostle Paul. These shifts can go positive to negative or vice versa. Again the shift from thinking negatively to positively is a reframe that causes a shift in opinion and feelings about the other person or subject. These examples have illustrated in a negative way what happens in counseling when a reframe connects within a counselee.

To illustrate that reframing can switch from positive to negative, consider that there are situations that are better managed by assisting people in seeing their behavior in a negative, foolish, or pointless frame. Milton Erickson illustrates the negative reframe.

> My son, Bert, at the manly age of five . . . feeling his importance as a citizen, said, "I'm not going to eat any of THAT stuff!!" . . . referring to a bowl of spinach. And I said, "Of COURSE not. You're not old enough, not strong enough, not big enough!" Mother started protesting, "He is TOO old enough, big enough, strong enough." And you know on whose side Bert was.[12]

Suddenly eating spinach took on an entirely different meaning, and nothing was changed other than the words or frame that defined eating or not eating.

> To reframe, then, means to change the conceptual and/or emotional setting or viewpoint in relation to which a situation is experienced and to place it in another frame which fits the "facts" of the same concrete situation equally well or even better, and thereby changes its entire meaning. What

turns out to be changed as a result of reframing is the meaning attributed to the situation, and therefore its consequences but not its concrete facts—or, as the philosopher Epictetus expressed it as early as the first century A.D., "It is not the things themselves which trouble us, but the opinion that we have about these things."[13]

Reframing changes the classification of an object, behavior, feeling, and/or thought. Classifications are arbitrary and rarely mutually exclusive; therefore, shifting from one class to another is very possible and often very therapeutic.[14] In counseling, reframing can change how people view others, and make it difficult for them to return to the old pathological way of thinking. For example, troubled families identify one member of the family as the problem person whose behavior is classified as either bad/naughty or crazy/sick. The bad/naughty person willfully acts contrary to the rules of the family, but the crazy/sick person is unable to behave otherwise due to some infirmity.[15] Reframing changes these limiting frames in a positive rather than negative way. In an earlier chapter, when resistance was reframed as persistence, a positive category shift, the counselor was able to think better of the counselee.

Taking on another person's view of the problem may doom the therapeutic process, but the ability to see in the dysfunctional behavior how the person tried to cope with some difficulty opens the possibility of reframing the problem behavior in a more useful way. For example, a quarreling couple is actually very committed to each other, and their quarreling illustrates how important communicating is to each of them.[16]

Effective reframing also touches feelings. To reframe quarreling as trying to get closer to the other person changes the emotional climate that encourages the couple to feel and to care again. Believing the other person wants to communicate softens the hardened relationship and helps the feelings to flow between them again. The fact that they quarrel does not change, but the meaning, as defined by the reframe behind the quarreling, does change.

LEVELS OF CHANGE AND POWER OF REFRAME

Bartunek and Moch outline three levels of change: the first uses problem-solving skills; the second involves a therapeutic reframe of the situation presented in such a way that the counselee begins to act differently; and the third helps people reframe situations for themselves.[17] Self-reframing is a powerful step that potentially frees counselees from the need for a counselor.[18] Those who learn to reframe for themselves turn problem situations into opportunities for growth and better health. Therefore, because shifting frames opens many additional alternatives and solutions, counselors can teach reframing during the counseling process as one of the problem-solving skills.

The findings of one researcher illustrate the power of reframing. He discovered that children, even though they denied the positive reframe, could not ignore it and were thereby influenced to significantly change their behavior.[19] The power of reframing rests on its believableness, appropriateness, and fit. Insincere reframes seem manipulative and deceptive, a condition working directly against healthy therapeutic interaction.[20] If the reclassification of an object, feeling, behavior, or thought is not believable, the counselee will likely call it a lie and not benefit from it. An appropriate reframe takes people out of the quagmire of one frame and places them into a solvable or healthier frame. A powerful reframe makes sense to the counselee and lifts him or her out of the unhealthy frame.

Reframing puts the observer above the problem. When Christ's antagonizers asked about the morality of paying taxes to Caesar, Jesus reframed the situation by asking them to identify the image on the coin (Matt. 12:13–17). "Caesar's," they replied, opening the door for Jesus' instruction to give to Caesar that which belonged to Caesar and to God that which belonged to God. Simply stated, the reframe put Jesus above the situation, for He was not trapped in the apparent contradiction as the antagonists wanted.[21]

Kraft, et al. found positive reframing a significant influencer of client mood as measured by the Beck Depression Inventory

(BDI) and a mood scale.[22] Those who received positive reframing statements scored significantly higher on the BDI and mood scale than those who received no reframing statements. There are two reasons for this. First, positive reframing nullifies the self-blame usually accompanying awareness of problems, and second, positive reframing gets the person to see life and the specific problem situation positively, which stimulates the client to look for more positive experiences. For example, have you noticed how many red traffic signals you encounter when you are in a hurry? You may even predict that, because you are in a hurry, the traffic lights will make you even later and that there will be more of them than usual. Because you have a negative perspective, you focus more on the red lights than the green lights. Chance is the only controlling variable in such cases, and you are just as likely to get a red light as a green light no matter how much you hurry.

Labeling people may have unhealthy consequences. When a problem arises, people are often identified as having the problem, and later they are viewed as being the problem. Such a label denigrates by classifying them in such a way that they also begin to view themselves as a problem. Positive reframing removes such a stigma and allows people to look at themselves in a positive and accepting manner, an attitude generating healthier interaction with themselves and the world.

CONTRASTING REFRAME, INTERPRETATION, AND RELABEL

Reframing differs from relabeling, giving advice, and psychotherapeutic interpretation. A relabel changes the name/label ascribed to a behavior, feeling, or thought. Changing a woman's label for her husband from fishy to flexible provided a relabeling that not only gave her a new way to view her husband's behavior, but so completely spoiled her old way of demeaning him that she was unable to return to it. Relabeling highlights the positive nature of the symptom and recasts it as friendly, whereas giving advice points out a wrong and asks for a change in the problem behavior.[23] Reframing goes beyond relabeling by taking a behavior, thought, or feeling and shifting it to a new category. The reframe is not as specific as relabeling. A styrofoam coffee cup could also be reframed as a cup to start seedlings, a container for sugar, and many other things. While relabeling takes a specific name or label and replaces it with another specific name or label, reframing deals with concepts and categories.

A therapeutic interpretation brings into awareness features of behavior that have not been evident so far. Interpretation differs from reframing in that, first, reframing ascribes new meaning aimed at the process, while interpretation aims at bringing the counselee to a different understanding *based on the theoretical orientation of the counselor*. Second, there are *many* possible reframes, but only *one* interpretation which follows the counselor's theoretical orientation. Third, the goal of interpretation is increased insight, which eventually leads to behavioral change; reframing's goal seeks an immediate change of behavior. Finally, reframing is pragmatic and process oriented, but therapeutic interpretation is oriented more toward content and insight.[24]

Changing perception from one frame to another is a reframe. This is in contrast to what O'Hanlon calls a deframe, a statement that destroys the original attributed meaning but does not offer a substitute meaning.[25] Counselees are left to create their own new frame or not to have any frame which may dissolve the problem altogether. In casual conversation we often deframe by challenging how a person looks at the facts without giving them a new perspective. When someone is hurting, well-wishers commonly say that there is no reason for the hurt, "You're just misreading the facts." Such an approach is a deframe because it offers no alternative frame.

According to de Shazer, dismantling a problematic frame involves accepting it, then inspecting it until an illogical or inconsistent place is found and the inconsistency pointed out to the client.[26] Inconsistency means that something the client tries to accomplish is not fulfilled if the logical conclusion of the frame comes true. For example, de Shazer reports treating a twenty-eight-year-old man who had been declaring since he was eight years old that he was the Devil, a belief that evoked from others logical and imploring arguments to the contrary. These arguments consistently failed, and the client experienced long hospital stays and medical treatments that he now wanted to avoid. De Shazer accepted the I-am-the-Devil frame and pointed out to the client that he, de Shazer, would be very angry if others did not believe him. However, the client declared that he now knew how he would prove he was the Devil, by perpetrating the vilest act he could imagine—nuclear holocaust. Again de Shazer agreed that such an act would prove he was the Devil, but wondered how that would be satisfying since there would be no one alive to grovel and agree. "Throughout this statement . . . Mr. F sat motionless, eyes wide open and unblinking."[27] The session concluded and was followed by three more sessions centering on getting off medication, getting out of the halfway house, and securing a job, all of which were successfully accomplished in the four sessions with no further therapy required.

Perhaps the reader wonders how a life-long problem could dissolve so quickly and easily. The prisoner who believed he had a low IQ changed instantly when Corsini described him as having a high IQ, a reclassification that shattered the old ways of behaving and instituted alterations resulting in his parole. Most of us can remember changes in thinking, feeling, and/or behavior because we came to understand ourselves differently. We probably would call this change an insight, but whatever word we use to label what happens, the mechanism is the same.

LIMITATIONS

Reframing does have several limitations as itemized by Jessee, et al.[28] Children who have not yet developed the logical ability to classify objects are unlikely to be able to reclassify as required in reframing. This limits the usefulness of reframing with children of approximately eight years or younger. Second, the purpose of reframing must be therapeutic and not just managerial, although such a distinction is often difficult in a residential setting. Third, reframing presupposes a caring relationship between the counselor and counselee, but this does not exclude the use of the reframe during earlier phases of counseling if the counselee senses the empathy of a skilled counselor. Finally, it is important to note that in a hospital setting the reframe may significantly influence the individual's behavior but will often result in regression after the person returns to the family system and its dysfunctional ways.

Seltzer describes the family characteristics that bode well for the use of reframing. These include a capacity for reflection and insight, only moderate crises, and rigid structures but only moderate resistance to change. These are situations where power struggles do not dominate in therapy.[29]

APPLICATION

Getting people to think of the symptom as a friend reframes the problem in a way that makes it useful. Ask, for example, "If the depression could talk, what would it say?" The symptom is not some unwanted experience but a signal warning of the need for a change such as taking more time, thinking about something else, stopping for a break, being with someone.

We can illustrate this idea by asking the counselee, "What would you do if you became short of breath while out jogging?" Slow down is the common-sense answer because the shortness of breath, a symptom of too much exertion, is merely a signal telling a person to take it easy. Life is full of such warnings, and we must help individuals get a benign perspective on them so they can make full use of what the symptom means by getting at the problem triggering the response.

REFRAMING DEPRESSION

Depression warns us that something is not working correctly in life. Depression demands attention. Sally, for instance, reported in somewhat confused terms how depressed she was feeling. She did not recognize her symptoms as depression but did realize that something was wrong—she felt sad and irritable, had problems sleeping, was experiencing a loss of appetite, and life just did not seem fun any longer. She could not pinpoint when the depression started, but she knew it had lasted several weeks.

During the interview, I wrote four words on a pad: depressed, disillusioned, discouraged, and disappointed.[30] I explained to her how depression often begins with disappointments, some of which are small but frequent while others may be large but less frequent, like the loss of a friend or job. I made sure she understood what I meant by disappointments. Then I explained that after being disappointed for a while it is easy to become discouraged, then disillusioned with oneself because others are not feeling this way; and finally, depression hits the body so that there are physical as well as emotional symptoms. The frame I built gave me room to discuss different aspects of depression and to ask her where she thought she was on the ladder of depression. No matter what step she selected I went directly to disappointments and asked her what the recent major disappointments in her life had been. When she had trouble identifying any disappointments, I helped her by defining a disappointment as the difference between what we expect and what actually happens. Writing these disappointments on the pad, I discussed them to help her get a full understanding of what was happening in her life. A discussion of this kind helped her tell her story and allowed me to express empathy. Reframing depression as disappointment permitted the problem to be treated directly.

Next, I found out how she had worked to overcome her depression. This information revealed what she thought about her problem and what means she had invoked to solve it. Attempted solutions revealed her style of coping with life, which was usually adequate, but for some reason did not work this time. Perhaps her coping style was causing more problems. It could be that her style of coping had kept her on the verge of depression for some time, and it was only lately that her mood had worsened. Answers to these questions began to form as we discussed the details of the problem and her way of coping with it.

When the counselor views the coping style as positive, the counselee does not feel judged, and relaxes and joins the counselor in solving the problem. If counselees feel judged they may become defensive and resist treatment. It is critical to reframe the coping style as positive despite the not-so-positive aspects— perhaps it was just too much of a good thing. For example, some people cope by withdrawing from conflict. Sometimes this is appropriate, but not always. Because a reframe changes one's perspective, it does not have to be shared with the counselee to be effective. For example, the counselor in the above example was significantly influenced by just seeing the other person in a positive way. A change in perspective stirs feelings and draws the counselor and counselee together.

I reframed twice in dealing with Sally: first, I reframed depression as disappointment; and second, I reframed her coping style as positive but overworked. It should be added, of course, that depression is a complex emotional and physical problem which must not be underestimated, especially when people are considering suicide. Some depressed people need immediate medical attention, and a medical examination is a reasonable request for anyone who has suffered from emotional symptoms for several weeks.

EMOTIONS ARE OK

Emotions are not right or wrong; they indicate emotional and physical health. Getting people to appreciate their feelings means providing a reframe that helps them pay attention rather than deny what is happening emotionally. Most people would not ignore a warning light on the car dashboard, but would quickly determine the difficulty before major damage to the engine occurred.

People acquainted with biblical interpretation know that once a text is interpreted it is very difficult to see it in any other way. Unfortunately this is also the case with interpretations of human behavior, feelings, and thoughts. Once people look at a thought or feeling as depressed, anxious, crazy, or sick, they have a difficult time viewing it any other way. Perceptive permanence works for the counselor because once the counselor makes the reclassification, it is very difficult for the counselee to go back to seeing the "thing" in the old way. Reframing spoils old interpretations and drags the counselee into a new consciousness promising, if the reframe is well conceived, better health.[31]

"'Psychological problems' are simply unfortunate ways of understanding or reframing a situation,"[32] and reframing people's experiences as normal serves to change how they view a situation. Once an abnormal label or conclusion is formed, whether true or false, all subsequent behavior is viewed as supporting that frame because people usually ignore all behaviors that are contrary to the frame. When a counselor says, "That seems pretty normal because . . . ," the original frame is weakened by being doubted, leaving room for a new, more healthy frame.

A male client was suffering from obsessive thoughts about people having horrible experiences such as one might see on TV or at the movies. He was relieved when his therapist pointed out how lucky the client was. "Most people have to go to the movies to get such ghoulish thrills." With this simple reframe the counselor normalized the client's experience, greatly relieving its painful consequences, strength, and repetitiveness. The counselor reframed the obsession as something other normal people paid to see.

Because of the plethora of self-help books, people often come to conclusions or interpretations about their problems that are not useful in solving the problem. Causally linking one's behavior to low self-esteem, a common conclusion, makes improving self-esteem the therapeutic task instead of changing behavior. Self-esteem is a label psychologists use to summarize how people think and feel about themselves, but it is not directly treatable, so it should be disconnected from any previously attributed interpretation or assumed cause. Counseling should address the beliefs and behaviors that actually cause the low self-esteem.

Low self-esteem may yield to a reframe that contaminates counselees' right to put themselves down. Ask counselees if they are prejudiced. Usually they emphatically deny prejudice, to which I reply that I can prove they are prejudiced. Such a statement challenges them to prove me wrong, and the harder they try the better. When the pressure reaches its greatest level I show them that they are prejudiced against themselves. Surprise illuminates their faces as they realize the negative impact of what they do to themselves, something they would not do to any other person. The force of their insistence about not being prejudiced is turned on their own attitude, which may then change enough to release them.

"Successful reframing must lift the problem out of the 'symptom' frame and into another frame that does not carry the implication of permanence. Of course, not just any other frame will do, but only one that is congenial to the person's way of thinking and of categorizing reality."[33] Jethro did this for Moses when he suggested that Moses enlist others to *help* judge the Israelites. Asking Moses to turn *all* judging over to others was contrary to his understanding of God's will, and he would have certainly refused.

How to Reframe

In reframing, counselors take what people bring to counseling and use that to help them solve their problem. For example, a demanding husband might be reframed as a concerned person willing to assist his wife in making the changes he wants her to make. To help her he must respond differently, so why not respond in a way that is more pleasing to his wife? By finding a common frame that meets both their needs, the counselor releases resources from within the husband and the wife.

This example illustrates what O'Hanlon and Wilk look for— a larger context into which the problem context and the solution context fit like two peas in a pod. They say, "In reframing, we find a descriptive abstraction (i.e. a label) that applies equally to the problem context and the 'native' context (i.e. general context), and so provides a more general description of both, so that they can be described as two versions of the same thing."[34]

Reframing encourages the transfer of skills and knowledge from one compartment of life to another. For example, a counselor encountered a woman whose marriage was in serious difficulty because she avoided conflict with her husband by withdrawing from him. This irritated the husband and he expressed his irritation as anger toward his wife. This in turn drove her further from him. When the counselor learned of her business experience in dealing with unhappy customers, the counselor connected these untapped resources with her need to deal more effectively with her husband's anger. The counselor pointed out the similarity between the two situations, reframing the marriage difficulty in such a way that her skills in business would transfer and ameliorate the marital discord. This was not a final solution, but a new beginning that made a difference in the marriage.

Global frames provide general conclusions. This is in contrast to specific frames, which make concrete interpretations about people and events. Global frames supersede any change in a specific frame.[35] Concluding or framing a child as a liar does not change when the child tells the truth on a specific occasion. When framed as a liar, he may tell the truth one time, but according to the frame, he is generally a liar. Therefore, he will lie again, a prophecy likely to be self-fulfilling. As long as the general frame exists, the parent communicates the general belief and encourages the child to lie again. Therefore, reframing general or broad frames should be done before reframing narrow or specific ones. Questioning the conclusion that the child is a liar is critical because the frame affects everything the child says, whether true or false, and because it implies there is something inherently wrong with the child. These kinds of implications are nearly impossible to overcome until the general frame, "He is a liar," is removed.

REFRAMING THE UNCHANGEABLE

Lying is amenable to change, but numerous conditions and situations exist that cannot be changed. These are also treatable by reframing—in fact, reframing may be the only possible treatment. A case reported by Watzlawick, et al., illustrates the effectiveness of reframing when the facts of the situation are not changeable.[36] A man with a stammering problem was forced to take a job as a salesman, but he realized that selling required the smooth and continuous flow of persuasive speech. The counselors pointed out to him that people listen very carefully to an individual with a speech problem, and that he might even wish to make his stammering worse so that people would pay even closer attention to his sales pitch. With such a reframe, the immutable speech problem was transformed into an asset.

In the first century slavery was common, and undoubtedly the slave would have considered himself a very low class of person with a resulting low sense of personal importance and value. The Apostle Paul encouraged slaves to think about their position in life in a different and healthier way: "Whatever you do, work at it with all your heart, as working for the Lord, not for men, since you know that you will receive an inheritance from the Lord as a reward. It is the Lord Christ you are serving" (Col. 3:23–24). Paul's reframe put the slaves' position into a different category and liberated them from the negativism associated with servitude.

Milton Erickson reported treating a young girl who exhibited high levels of anger toward almost everyone. Her mother told him that the girl had a very freckled face, and this prompted regular teasing from other children, resulting in self-hatred. When the girl came into the room, Erickson said,

> "You're a thief! You steal!"
>
> She said she was not a thief and she did not steal. She could do battle on that score.
>
> "Oh, yes, you're a thief. You steal things. I even know what you stole. I even have *proof* that you stole."
>
> She said, "You haven't got proof. I never stoled nothin'."
>
> I said, "I even know *where* you were when you stoled what you stole."
>
> That girl was thoroughly angry with me. I said, "I'll tell you where you were and what you stole. You were in the kitchen, setting the kitchen table. You were standing at the kitchen table. You were reaching up to the cookie jar, containing cinnamon cookies, cinnamon buns, cinnamon rolls—and you spilled some cinnamon on your face—you're a Cinnamon Face." [Erickson had learned from the mother that the little girl especially liked cinnamon.][37]

This reframe successfully challenged her perception of herself and resulted in a much happier and more pleasant child.

In another case, an eleven-year-old girl apparently had an irreversible bed-wetting problem, the result of cystoscopic treatments over several years for a persistent bladder infection. The resultant bed-wetting embarrassed her and limited her social opportunities. Erickson asked her what she would do if a man stuck his head into her rest room stall. She replied that she would freeze. Erickson reminded her that freezing would stop her from urinating and told her to practice imagining such an experience as a means of facilitating her bladder control. With excellent results Erickson took what would happen in one context and transferred it to the target context. Within a few weeks she was continent, and by six months she was staying overnight at the home of a friend.

SOCIAL IMPLICATIONS

Alfred Adler believed that all behavior has a social purpose—that we do what we do in order to get other people to do what we want them to do. Reframing is better understood as a means of improving social relationships. As noted earlier, the first social relationship to be influenced is the one between the reframer and the client. The counselor-reframer is significantly influenced by the reframe even before it is announced to the client. The client, following the announcement of the reframe, is catapulted into a better social context because problem behavior is now defined as socially meaningful and appropriate.

In addition, symptomatic behavior attempts to equalize an imbalance in the established interpersonal relationship system. *System imbalance* results when one or more members of an interpersonal system approach the current frame exerting either more or less control than is necessary or appropriate.[38] Pastors and other leaders know of system imbalances of the kind that often destroy the harmony of a board or committee and sometimes a whole church. Reframing tends to equalize the members of the interpersonal system and restore *system balance* by moving each member toward the normal, comfortable manner of each individual's style of behavior and control.[39]

EASING RESISTANCE

In more than one sense this form of problem resolution (reframing) is similar to the philosophy and technique of judo, where the opponent's thrust is not opposed by a counter thrust of at least the same force, but rather accepted and amplified by yielding to and going with it. This the opponent does not expect; he is playing the game of force against force, of more of the same, and by the rules of his game he anticipates a counter thrust and not a different game altogether.[40]

Resistance, illustrated in the principles of judo, often becomes a power struggle requiring at least two people to maintain, for when one person of the dyad changes position, the struggle ends. Positive reframing, with its paradoxical effect, dissolves the nature of the power struggle by using the counselee's opposing energy to change how the counselee views and behaves relative to the problem.[41] Reframing stems resistance.

Typically, once I have established the life style of a counselee, I attempt to reframe what some people would consider ineffective or wrong behavior. For example, I often see people who cause relational problems by withdrawing from conflict rather than facing and solving it. When I point out their style, I describe their behavior as an attempt to cooperate with others by giving all their resources away, an approach to life that developed in the past for some useful purpose but is now unnecessary. Usually this approach helps counselees relax and accept their styles while considering whether they want to add other styles.

Parents often encourage resistance by nagging and punishing to restrain thumb-sucking in their children. They fail to recognize the power of reframing by pointing out to the thumb sucker that in a democratic society, where everyone is recognized, it is unthinkable that only one finger should receive all of the attention. When parents insist that all the fingers get equal time measured by the clock, the sucking takes on a meaning far less reinforcing than nagging and punishing.[42]

Dennis Gibson generated a number of generic reframes that may apply to various problems. The following summarizes some of these.

"Labor pains" signal the beginning of something new in a person's life, and therefore herald change.

"Inoculations" give us antibodies against diseases, and the troubles of life are like inoculations which help us handle larger difficulties in the future.

In a similar way "Boot Camp" prepares the raw recruit to face battle, and the boot camp of life readies people for other subsequent difficulties.

"Thanksgiving," a powerful exercise of faith, encourages people to look for the God-designed way of taking a difficulty and turning it into good.

"Observers" of life have a different perspective from the participants, and assigning people the non-miserable observer role of noting only what is happening may take them beyond the immediate pain.

Just as a "Test Pilot" takes a plane to its limits, so a child may try his parents' love to find its limit and therefore its security.

For people who are concerned about being too heavy handed with their families, you can reframe the situation by helping them distinguish between authoritarian and authoritative. "'Authoritarian' leadership is harsh, heavy-handed, inconsiderate, concerned only with compliance of the governed, not their well being. 'Authoritative' means kind, clear, dependably holding firm—because of a concern for the well-being of the governed. A leader can be authoritative without being authoritarian."

A woman, who had grown up with very critical parents, was reframed as hibernating instead of withdrawing, a change of classification which stuck with her husband allowing him to treat her differently.[43]

In these generic reframes Gibson provides examples that might be used regularly, but the reader must approach each counseling situation as unique, and any generic reframe needs tailoring to fit different counselees and situations. Let all of the examples of reframing throughout this chapter serve as models of and prompts for creative effort within your own principles.

BIBLICAL EXAMPLES

Although the Bible does not address reframing directly, it contains numerous examples of reframing. Perhaps the clearest example is found in James 1:1–4 where James reframes trials as an opportunity to experience joy because trials work in behalf of the sufferer. While we usually view trials as something to avoid, we can now, if we take James's reframe, actually benefit from them. Aren't we just whitewashing the fact that pain is objectionable and to be avoided? Not at all, for we must remember that reframes that are not true are rejected by the receiver and are suspect of being unethical. James is making a valid point about gaining valuable lessons and experience from trials.

I look into my own life to illustrate what James is saying. In spite of my not rejoicing in trials, I have benefited from hard experiences. In 1970 Brenda, my wife, became symptomatic with Systemic Lupus Erythematosus (SLE), a very serious, disabling disease which could be fatal—at the time we did not know for sure. I struggled with this trial and found it very difficult to call it joyful, but as I look back over the more than twenty years since 1970, we have learned much about patience, supporting others, faith, caring, and understanding others when they hurt. Without faith and God's perspective, trials are just pain that should be avoided at all costs. James gives us a frame that opens a window on the future and a glimpse of what can come from even the most hurtful experiences.

Paul also illustrates how trials build strength of character into the sufferer (Rom. 5:3–5; 2 Cor. 1:3–11). The severe trials Paul enumerated increased his ability to comfort others. He learned to comfort with the same comfort he had received from God. Not the trials but the character development is worth rejoicing over, because we know God works all things together for our good (Rom. 8:28–29).

King Solomon startled people when he switched the frame placed on a surviving baby claimed by two mothers (1 Kings 3:16–27). As long as everyone thought of the baby as a human being they were caught between the claims of the two mothers. But when Solomon reframed the baby as a thing, an expendable, the real mother stepped forward to reveal herself.

The way out of these kinds of traps is not the obvious way, for escape lies in a direction that seems absurd and contrary to common sense. Throughout the ages, God has reframed people and situations to bring out the best in both.

Consider how God views sinners before and after they have appropriated salvation. Nothing in the sinner has changed, but there is a total difference in how God views the sinner. This eternal reframe is consistent with God's character and purpose in the world. Yet this one-of-a-kind reframe envelopes the totality of history and eternity, and is so unusual that only God could conceive and execute it.

Reframing is an important component of short-term counseling. Its nonsensical impact startles the counselee into a new way of viewing life. The durability of the change is assured by the appropriateness and truthfulness of the reframe. Without reframing, short-term counseling would lose a powerful technique for bringing relief to people.

CONCLUSION

This chapter reviews what some have considered an elegant intervention in the lives of people trapped by how they view life. Reframing addresses one of the things that can change in the consulting room: how people view their problems. When perspective is challenged and changed, what people think and do will change also.

NOTES

1. Robert Fulghum, *All I Really Need to Know I Learned in Kindergarten* (New York: Ivy Books, 1989), 4–5.

2. Paul Watzlawick, James Weakland, and Richard Fisch, *Change: Principles of problem formation and problem resolution* (New York: Norton, 1974), 96–97.

3. See Bill O'Hanlon and James Wilk, *Shifting Contexts: The generation of effective psychotherapy* (New York: Guilford, 1987), 17–23; and William O'Hanlon, *Taproots: Underlying principles of Milton Erickson's therapy and hypnosis* (New York: Norton, 1987), 96.

4. O'Hanlon, *Taproots*, 54–66.

5. S. I. Hayakawa, *Language in Thought and Action*, 4th ed. (New York: Harcourt Brace Jovanovich, 1978), 153.

6. Ibid. p. 152–70.

7. Watzlawick, Weakland, and Fisch, *Change*, 95–96.

8. Paul Watzlawick, *The Language of Change: Elements of therapeutic communication* (New York: Basic Books, 1978), 120.

9. Yvonne Dolan, *A Path with a Heart: Ericksonian utilization with resistant and chronic clients* (New York: Bruner/Mazel, 1985), 91.

10. O'Hanlon, *Taproots*, 96–98.

11. Dennis Gibson, *Vitality Therapy* (Grand Rapids, Mich.: Baker Book House, 1989), 57.

12. D. Gordon and M. Meyers–Anderson, *Phoenix: Therapeutic patterns of Milton H. Erickson* (Cupertino, Calif.: Meta Publications, 1981), 81.

13. Watzlawick, Weakland, and Fisch, *Change*, 95.

14. Ibid. p. 97.

15. Linda LaClave and Gregory Brack, "Reframing to deal with patient resistance: Practical application," *American Journal of Psychotherapy* 43, no. 1 (January 1989), 68.

16. LaClave and Brack, "Reframing," 69–70.

17. J. M. Bartunek and M. K. Moch, "First-order, second-order, third-order change and organization development interventions: A cognitive approach," *Journal of Applied Behavioral Science* 23 (1988), 483–500.

18. LaClave and Brack, "Reframing," 69.

19. Edgar Jessee, et al., "Positive reframing with children: Conceptual and clinical considerations," *American Journal of Orthopsychiatry* 52, no. 2 (April 1982), 317.

20. Stephen Lankton and C. Lankton, *The Answer Within: A clinical framework of Ericksonian hypnotherapy* (New York: Bruner/Mazel, 1983), 338.

21. Watzlawick, Weakland, and Fisch, *Change*, 95.

22. Robert Kraft, Charles Claiborn, and E. Thomas Dowd, "Effects of positive reframing and paradoxical directives in counseling for negative emotions," *Journal of Counseling Psychology* 32, no. 4 (1985), 620.

23. Angelo Puig, "Relabeling or restructuring as a supportive therapeutic intervention in problems of academic stress," *Journal of College Student Personnel* (May 1983), 273–74.

24. L. Michael Ascher, ed. *Threapeutic Paradox* (New York: Guilford, 1989), 327–28.

25. O'Hanlon, *Taproots*, 98–99.

26. Steve de Shazer, *Clues: Investigating solutions in brief therapy* (New York: Norton, 1988), 101–03.

27. de Shazer, *Clues*, 107.

28. Jessee, et al., "Positive Reframing," 320–21.

29. L. Seltzer, *Paradoxical Strategies in Psychotherapy: A comprehensive overview and guidebook* (New York: John Wiley & Sons, 1986), 238–39.

30. Starting to write at the bottom of the paper allows the full impact of what is triggering the depression to break into the counselee's cognition. My

personal style of counseling involves frequent use of drawings which illustrate what the counselee is trying to understand and resolve.

31. Watzlawick, Weakland, and Fisch, *Change*, 95.

32. Milton H. Erickson, in *Life Reframing in Hypnosis: The Seminars, Workshops, and Lectures of Milton H. Erickson*, vol. 2, ed. E. L. Rossi and O. M. Ryan (New York: Irvington, 1985), xiv.

33. Watzlawick, Weakland, and Fisch, *Change*, 102–3.

34. O'Hanlon and Wilk, *Shifting Contexts*, 136.

35. de Shazer, Clues, 103–4

36. Watzlawick, Weakland, and Fisch, *Change*, 94–95.

37. Sidney Rosen, ed., *My Voice Will Go With You: The teaching tales of Milton H. Erickson, M.D.* (New York: Norton, 1982), 152–53.

38. Warren Heard, *Second-Order Cybernetics and the Teachings of Jesus* (Unpublished manuscript, 1990).

39. Gerald Weeks and Luciano L'Abate, *Paradoxical Psychotherapy: Theory and practice with individuals, couples, and families* (New York: Bruser/Mazel, 1982), 90–91.

40. Watzlawick, Weakland, and Fisch, *Change*, 104.

41. Jessee, et al., "Positive Reframing," 317. They found this holds true with children in therapy.

42. Watzlawick, *Language of Change*, 121.

43. Gibson, *Vitality Therapy*, 41–63.

Chapter Eleven

Paradox in Counseling

In THE EIGHTEENTH CENTURY a man reported to his physician that he had no head. The physician responded by trying to fill up the "empty" space with a large lead ball. The ensuing pain convinced the deluded man that he did have a head after all.[1] Sound crazy? Contrary to common sense? Often uncommon sense springs the trapped counselee out of the psychological snare. In chapter 1 we reported a case involving a woman who thought someone had placed in her ear a listening device that transmitted her speech and, sometimes, thoughts to others. She demonstrated the tenacity of her belief by refusing to say aloud her phone number. I treated this case very much like the one above, taking the belief to its logical conclusion and convincing her that the belief was wrong.

I told this woman that I was very curious about such a listening device because my father worked for years in the field of electronics. By asking her how she thought the device was powered and listing the possibilities (we concluded it must be battery powered since solar power required sunlight and house current calls for a wire), I challenged its logical reality and gave her an alternate view which disturbed the belief. Furthermore, I expressed concern that she might grow dependent on such a device for getting her thoughts across to other people, a result she should guard herself against.

At the second interview I continued in a similar manner to challenge her belief, and in the third interview I expressed some jealousy about not having such a device myself to help get my thoughts across to people. She responded by waving her hand at me and saying, "Oh, you!" Although she continued in counseling for other issues, from then on she did not mention the listening device. Her interests turned to real concerns of work, retirement, grandchildren, and other incidental considerations.

These examples illustrate the use of paradox in counseling. In a paradox the counselor asks the client to do two things simultaneously, one obvious and intriguing, the other less obvious but powerful and therapeutic.[2] For example, telling a thumb-sucking child that it is undemocratic to suck just the thumb and to suck each digit the same amount of time as recorded strictly by the minute and second hands of a strategically placed clock, is the obvious and curious message; the less obvious message is: suck at the counselor's direction and timing. Within all of us something wants to rebel against being told what to do, and rebellion in the thumb-sucker would result in not sucking at all.

THEORY OF THERAPEUTIC PARADOX

By now you may be wondering how therapeutic paradoxes work. What is the theory behind them? Stubborn independence that results in rebellion is an obvious, but not necessarily the best, explanation for therapeutic paradox. For example, consider what happens when you try (sometimes with all your might) to drive an unwanted thought from your mind. Most people report that the persistence of the unwanted thought is highly correlated with the level of effort to drive it out. This happens because trying not to think about a thought demands thinking about it, that is, by concentrating on ridding ourselves of the unwanted thought we force ourselves to focus on it anyway. Who can keep the tongue from going to a sore spot in the mouth? The tongue of the mind continues to search out the unwanted thought regardless of any injunctions against doing so.

The effectiveness of paradoxical interventions is supported by numerous reports of counselors who successfully use these techniques in their practices, but the use of paradoxical procedures is not limited or attached to any particular theory of counseling. In fact, just the opposite appears to be true. Most, if not all, therapy models use paradoxical interventions. Seltzer devotes an entire book to a discussion of the appearance of paradoxical interventions in the major counseling theories and practices.[3] There are some explanations based on existing theories. We develop these briefly here, but an in-depth discussion of how theories explain the success of paradoxical interventions lies beyond the purview of this book.

Symptoms may occur because the counselee strives too hard, and paradoxical interventions, usually humorous, interrupt this striving process. Watzlawick and other members of a group of brief therapists at the Mental Research Institute in Palo Alto, California, view symptoms as communication problems, that is, commands or demands made by members of the counselee's social group trigger symptomatic behavior. In a manner similar to the Palo Alto therapists, a group in Albany, New York, defines the symptom as reactance, an individual effort to maintain personal freedoms. Milton Erickson amends the counselee's problem behavior by creating an illusion of choice: "Which symptom do you want to work on first, insomnia or agoraphobia?" The question of whether the counselee would work on *any* symptom is taken for granted.

According to still another group of therapists (in Milan, Italy), symptomatic behavior results from the way a family interacts, and symptom prescription interrupts those rules and leaves the counselor in a winner's position. In other words, once the counselor prescribes the client to willfully act out the symptom; if the patient complies, this prepares the way for other changes; if the patient defies, this is the first step toward recovery. Either of these reactions breaks the family rules.

Weeks and L'Abate reframe the symptom as a friend which, rather than shunned, is welcomed and appreciated for its helpfulness in the past where it was created to serve some useful purpose.[4] Behavior therapists enjoin the client to have the behavior so steps can be taken to extinguish it.[5] Avoidance of responsibility, according to Gestalt therapists, generates the symptoms, and asking the counselee to exaggerate the symptom is an effort to tear down the defensive walls and expose the blocks and inhibitions to responsibility.

Reality therapy, developed by William Glasser, explains the success of paradoxical interventions as a disruption of the purpose of the problem behavior. If throwing a tantrum is designed for and rewarded by parental involvement, then having the parents encourage the child to have a tantrum disturbs its purpose and reduces the likelihood of its reoccurring.

Symptom prescription removes the support that encourages the problem to continue. By so doing, the context or frame which the symptom requires in order to continue is changed. Omer compares the elements of paradoxical intervention to the parts of a jigsaw puzzle.[6] The pieces that are fitted together provide the frame, support, and meaning of any individual piece which, when joined to the others, gives the whole its completeness. "The paradoxical intervention aims at bringing about symptom production while changing the mutual support between symptom and context."[7] For example, Joseph Fabry reports how a schoolboy who expressed his anger by breaking pencils and tearing up pads of paper was sent to the school counselor. After breaking several pencils at the counselor's suggestion, the boy exclaimed, "But this is ridiculous," and in one insight saw how foolish his angry behavior was. He returned to class noticeably different.[8] Asking for the symptom produces a paradoxical shift pushing the symptomatic person in a healthier direction.

AN EXAMPLE OF PARADOX FROM THE BIBLE

As recorded in John 8:1–11, the teachers and Pharisees brought to Jesus a woman caught in the act of adultery, a sin demanding stoning according to Mosaic Law. Their question, asking Jesus to decide if she should be stoned, was designed as a religious and political trap with no apparent escape. If Jesus said to stone her He would violate the law stating that only the Roman governor could issue a death sentence, and if He judged in her favor, He would violate Mosaic Law. Jesus eluded their trap by asking them to decide on the basis of their personal holiness. "Go ahead and stone her" tells them to do what the law requires. "Count your own sins" also fulfills the law because it emphasizes the spirit of the law, and that they could not deny. The cognitive dissonance generated by Jesus' challenge could only be relieved by withdrawing from the scene; so they did, starting with the older men who either were wiser than the younger men or had more sins to consider.

ETHICAL CONSIDERATIONS

Fabry comments on two objections to the concept of paradoxical intention first introduced by Frankl.[9] The first objection was that this short-term technique would have no effect on long-term problems. The second suggested that, because it only dealt with symptoms, it would not get at the deeper root problems. However, the evidence does not support either objection. Clinical success does not positively correlate with length of treatment. Short-term treatments result in long-term success just as frequently, if not more frequently, than long-term treatments. People treated with paradoxical intention remain symptom-free over several years with little or no further treatment, even when they face extreme stress.

Paradoxical interventions frequently come under fire for potential ethical violations, and these objections usually revolve around the paradox's apparent manipulative characteristics. The critics apparently fail to recognize the manipulative nature of all therapy that helps people become healthy through definite interventions. From the moment counselors answer the phone and continuing through all of the sessions some kind of manipulation is occurring. Perhaps the problem resides more in the pejorative insinuations connected with the word *manipulation* than in actual works of the counselor during the therapy process. Helping people make better choices for themselves hardly seems like manipulation in its worst sense. A better word for what occurs in counseling is *management* because the counselor's responsibility, even those who are committed to a nondirective approach, is to provide for people the best therapeutic atmosphere possible.

Another criticism of paradoxical interventions questions how genuine counselors are with their clients. People should be allowed to make a choice about what happens in counseling, say the critics, though these critics often fail to disclose the reasoning or procedures behind using other techniques, such as rapport. Rapport, like most procedures used in the consulting room, is a management technique designed to enhance the relationship between counselors and counselees. It would seem that all counseling is managerial in some sense. It is essential that we weigh other ethical issues such as keeping people in counseling (whether they pay or not) for extended periods. Considerations in length of counseling must be balanced with psychic pain and its relationship with the disruption of normal life patterns and financial cost.

Also consider that human management occurs outside counseling relationships. Even God manages people for their best interest. When God gave human beings a free will, He brought into existence the elements and process necessary for a paradoxical relationship to develop between Himself and humankind. The paradox created by commanding people to willingly surrender their free wills is comparable to altering people in order to create robots which would do what God wanted out of duty rather than love and devotion. But this was not God's intent, and it does not meet the requirement of willing surrender. God wants us to surrender to Him because we desire it, making unncessary any command to surrender. God has given us the solution to the paradox: unconditional love based on the effectual work of Christ on the cross, a sacrifice worthy enough to pay for the sins of the whole world. Most theories of counseling include unconditional acceptance as a basic ingredient for therapy to generate better health in the client. Unconditional acceptance is very similar to unconditional love. From the counselor's perspective unconditional love and acceptance are the only escapes from the paradox created by the clash of the wills of two free agents.

PARADOX FROM THE COUNSELEE'S PERSPECTIVE

How do therapeutic paradoxes work subjectively within people? First, the counselee subjectively realizes that the symptom is under voluntary control, and that recovery involves taking responsibility for dealing with the problem. Second, although therapeutic paradoxes do not challenge or change the underlying belief structure, they do move the belief toward absurdity and cause cognitive dissonance, which is the difficulty of entertaining contrary thoughts and theories. For example, once a paragraph is interpreted, a reader has difficulty accepting any other suggested meaning. Third, since the symptom is irrational ("I don't know or understand why I'm doing this, but . . ."), the solution is also not logical. In fact, the therapeutic paradox confuses the logical part of the counselee but stimulates the right hemisphere of the brain which is less logical in solving problems. Fourth, problem resolution is something like "catching on" to a joke or finding the way out without using a map.[10]

COGNITIVE DISSONANCE THEORY

Kercher and Smith use cognitive dissonance theory to explain how paradoxical interventions influence people.[11] The discomfort arising from the discrepancy between the contradictory aspects of the paradox is based on the theory of cognitive dissonance first formulated by Festinger in 1957.[12] It rests on the assumption that human beings need consistency and harmony within their cognitions (their thought patterns, perceptions, beliefs, etc.). When these contradictory patterns exist, they persistently work toward eliminating the discomfort that, if allowed to remain, generates anxiety. A directive calling for two incompatible responses creates dissonance. Consider the paradox presented in these statements: Don't everyone look at me; Speak up if you cannot hear me;

Be natural; Surrender your own free will; Tell me you love me, but only if you mean it; Be more domineering; Resist everything I tell you.[13]

Changes to established thought patterns do not necessarily consider the constraints or definitions of the real world, and distortions of reality are possible. The resistant quality of a cognition is directly related to the degree of clarity or ambiguity in the factual situation. This means that greater clarity results in a stronger, more resistant perception than one based on ambiguous evidence. Since resistant quality also depends on the recency of the formulations of the cognition, this resistance depends on the age of the belief, with older patterns being weaker than newer ones.

According to Kercher and Smith, the magnitude of dissonance relates to six factors.[14] The first factor notes that discomfort increases as the number of inconsistent cognitions grows; the second relates to the number of relevant consistent patterns—where there are fewer relevant perceptions, the cognitive dissonance is greater. The importance of the relevant consistent patterns and inconsistent cognitions is a third factor, while the fourth depends on the level of commitment. High levels of commitment influence perception and screen out or distort any further evidence that would influence the cognition. Dissonance also increases when the individual senses personal responsibility in the situation. To discern the elements of responsibility Kercher and Smith cite Goethals, et al., who break responsibility into foreseeability and choice.[15] "Finally, the dissonance experienced is related to awareness. The more conscious attention is directed toward the discrepant cognitive elements, the greater the dissonance experienced."[16]

The discomfort produced by the paradox can be changed by several means: eliminate or reduce the importance of inconsistent patterns; add or increase the importance of consistent cognitions; or lower the relevance of the inconsistent beliefs.

CHANGES AFFECTED BY PARADOX

Now let us consider how dissonance theory explains the kinds of changes resulting from paradoxical interventions.

Such interventions call for people to have or do the symptom by willing it. The impact of the prescription is directly related to increasing the counselee's sense of cognitive dissonance. Asking a person to practice the symptom is inconsistent, or dissonant, with the view that the symptom is something to be avoided. This prescription increases the counselee's responsibility and increases the level of dissonance which, in turn, can be reduced by several tactics.

One tactic discounts the qualifications of the counselor. This creates yet another inconsistency between the opinion of an incompetent counselor and the fee the counselee is paying. Resolving such a disharmony may mean terminating with the therapist or altering the attribution of incompetence. Changing his or her view of the counselor would lead back to the original therapeutic cognitive inconsistency and force the counselee to change how he or she views the symptom. The counselee would have to see it more positively, which would reduce the dissonant cognition. The only other option would be to change the behavior by adding consistent cognitions. Either way the person improves, the overall implied goal of counseling.

The successful therapeutic paradox also shifts the counselee's interpretation of the symptom from involuntary to voluntary, from uncontrollable to controllable, from determinism to freedom. O'Connell cites four indices of this type of therapeutic shift. First, the symptom appears as a solution to another problem (such as stress, a marital problem, or low self-esteem). Second, the counselee sees the absurdity, and thus humor, of how the symptom is supposed to solve the problem. The third is a shift from passivity to indignation and anger. For example, an anxious woman was asked to increase her anxiety for the following week, to which she responded with an anger that obviated her anxiety because she could not be angry and anxious at the same time. Fourth, the successful paradoxical intervention confuses, bewilders, or disorients the counselee. Bewilderment and confusion are incompatible with symptomatic behavior. These four indices signal that the paradox, the symptom prescription, has "taken."[17]

A pathological paradox binds the subject in such a way that he or she cannot be healthy no matter which alternative is chosen. For example, the parental command to be more spontaneous in your expression of affection has two alternatives: obey the command and sacrifice the spontaneity that disobeys the command, or disobey the command and be spontaneous, something that cannot happen by command. The person caught in such a paradox cannot win no matter which alternative is chosen.

In *Pragmatics of Human Communication* the authors cite this kind of pathological paradox as driving some young people into schizophrenic withdrawal.[18] In a pathological system, paradox operates on the family rule that no one may comment on the nature of the paradox itself. In other words, no one is permitted to say this is a paradoxical bind and attempt to make changes on a higher level. The pathological family typically has no way of talking about the rules themselves, or there is no amendment clause in the family constitution allowing for discussion of the rules by which the family operates.

Conversely, therapeutic paradox allows the counselee to win with either choice taken. Taking a symptom to its logical end forces the person to accept the counselor's leadership and thus submit to his or her control, or to reject the line of thought and spontaneously recover. Either alternative is healthier. For example, as extreme as this may seem, an alcoholic who drinks uncontrollably was told by his therapist to decide when and where his next drunk was to occur, how many drinks it would take, and to order more than enough drinks all at the same time, then to proceed deliberately to get drunk. Either the alcoholic rejects this command and maintains sobriety or follows it to drink on command, which, for this person is a different way of drinking. If the person can change any of the circumstances (e.g., when, where, how much) regarding drinking, he or she may be able to drink less.[19]

Paradox catches the observer between the frame and the content of the communication. For example, "All Cretans are liars" provides the frame or statement that defines Cretans in general and becomes paradoxical when a Cretan utters it, a specific example. The illogical gap between the frame and the specific content leaves the listener confused and unable to decide whether the frame is true or the speaker, a Cretan, is truthful. Both cannot be correct! Estimate the amount of confusion and damage done when a child who is labeled as a liar speaks the truth and is caught in the same paradox as the Cretan.

COMPLIANCE STRATEGIES

There are a couple of requirements to consider when implementing a paradoxical strategy. The first is a strong relationship between the counselor and the client. The second is the rationale the counselor gives the client for the odd assignment of increasing the problem or behavior he or she came to get rid of.

PARADOX REQUIRES A STRONG SOCIAL RELATIONSHIP

Therapeutic paradox, like any other technique, requires that the counselor and counselee have a strong social relationship developed by careful listening and accurate reflection of thoughts and feelings. To forsake the basics and go for the quick cure, without first building the proper social foundation, would likely end in failure.[20] Compliance is always more likely when there is a strong social relationship in the therapeutic dyad.

Good social relationships can grow rather quickly, even in the first session. Learning how to win people over early in the counseling process is critical in making use of paradoxical techniques. Chapter 5 discussed the building of therapeutic relationships. Watzlawick, et al., believe the counselor "has a rather limited period of grace in which to accomplish his goal."[21] They continue by underlining the tendency of a system to close around the counselor in such a way that change becomes very difficult. The best time for a symptom prescription is during the first session. This gives the client something to do, defines the therapy as problem solving, and places the counselor in charge. Timing and rapport, however, must mesh to provide the best opportunity to influence people.

RATIONALIZING THE PARADOX

Symptom prescription usually calls for giving the counselee some rationale for increasing the symptom. Summarized below are several approaches that O'Connell has enumerated:[22]

1. Get Drastic—You have tried everything to no avail; perhaps it's time to try something really different, like reverse psychology.

2. Develop Insight—To obtain some insight into just what is going on, I suggest in the next week you experiment by experiencing your symptom.

3. Collect Information—In order to get more information about your problem (depression, anxiety), I suggest you do some experimenting to discover more about the time, circumstances, and levels of response to your problem.

4. Change Strategies—I suggest you concentrate on your symptom so that you can try new ways of controlling it. This may include anything different from what you have been doing.

5. Assess Seriousness—To fully understand your problem, I suggest you intensify it this week so that I can get a full understanding of just what is going on. You may want to use the time just before your next appointment as one of those times so that you arrive here with the symptom and I can then see it for myself.

6. Run the Course—Occasionally problems develop because we do not allow them to run their course, and problems usually get worse before they get better. I suggest you intensify your problem so it can run its course more quickly, and you'll get through it sooner.

7. Have Fun—Problems often occur because we take things too seriously. I want you to intensify your problem so that you can see the absurd or humorous side of what you are doing.

8. Go Slowly—Solving a problem like yours requires time. Hurrying through the solution may trigger some other

problem that could be avoided if we are careful and de-liberate.

9. Take Charge—Your description of the problem clearly indicates how helpless you are. Your problem victimizes you, and I suggest you take charge of the symptom and learn how to control it.

10. Be Yourself—Your symptom makes you distinctive and unique. If you were to lose it you would no longer stand out in the crowd. So keep it up, and you may want to intensify the symptom to make yourself even more unique.

11. Explore the Irrational—Most problems like yours are the product of the irrational part of us. Treating your problem rationally is unlikely to solve it. So, try something really irrational like creating the problem on purpose, even intensify it to really emphasize the irrational nature of what you are doing.

O'Connell's rationales for symptom prescription illustrate how reframing and symptom prescription usually occur together, with the former providing the rationale for the latter. Reframing a symptom as useful allows for it to be turned into part of the treatment for the problem the person brings to you.

Be careful, however, to avoid paradoxical interventions that block further therapeutic options. Casting an intervention as an ultimatum reduces the counselor's options, while casting an intervention in the form of an experiment leaves room for failure and does not close off any future choices.[23] Making tentative suggestions is another useful way to avoid deadlocks with people. For example, asking people what happened when they tried a specific change allows them to report that they have not tried it and leaves the door open for them to consider trying it soon. Putting the suggestion in the form of what other people have found successful also approaches the intervention obliquely enough to avoid resistance. Rationales and approaches can vary with any counselor willing to push the limits of imagination.

PRINCIPLES FOR APPLYING PARADOXICAL INTERVENTIONS

Paradoxical interventions can be viewed in two ways. Such interventions can be looked at in terms of the objective sought. They can also be evaluated by their intensity.

APPLYING PARADOX BY OBJECTIVES

Driscoll recommends choosing paradoxical interventions by objectives rather than by treatment theory.[24]

Alleviating Pressure.   Pressure generated by performance-based behaviors such as impotence is best treated by asking the man to practice being impotent in a sexually stimulating situation but without having to engage in intercourse. Usually he is sufficiently stimulated to perform successfully.

Achieving Voluntary Control.   When a behavior or physical response is under unconscious control, asking the client to consciously produce the behavior usually removes its power to unconsciously control the individual, resulting in the freedom to either produce or not produce it consciously.

Eradicating Operating Beliefs.   Encouraging people to perform their unwanted behavior (assuming it is legal and safe) gives them the opportunity to discover whether the behavior accomplishes what they want. Asking inveterate worriers to worry even more, but to note how the worrying helps them, brings into question the belief that worrying can forestall a potential problem. This assignment can even ask for more worrying or worrying during a prescribed time period each day. Typically, people find it difficult to worry on schedule, so they worry less.

Legitimizing.   Giving people permission to keep their symptom often removes most of the fear. Telling the distrustful client that he or she has every right to be cautious legitimizes the person's distrust and helps build confidence in the counselor. The intervention could be worded: "I suggest that you take awhile before you open up to me so you can find out about me and see how much you can trust me."

Making Unacceptable Actions Conscious.   When people do things inconsistent with their own values, bringing the unacceptable actions into consciousness allows people to evaluate their behavior objectively. Telling someone who is getting even with another person how much right he or she has to get even releases the person to view such vengeful plans in light of his or her values. Such an unvarnished look at revenge is likely to end vengefulness.

Appealing to Individuality. Using resistance to draw people into doing what is best for them turns the table on them in a way that is nearly impossible to escape. This judo-like approach utilizes their resistance. A boy was brought to therapy because he was difficult and resistant to discipline. With his parent's permission, he was encouraged to be resistant so the counselor would have some material to make into a journal article. In addition, the parents were going to report on how he was doing so he would not even have to come to counseling himself. Highly surprised, the boy commented that he was not sure he was going to like this arrangement. He was trapped between helping the counselor with the article or resisting the counselor and behaving for his parents.

APPLYING PARADOX BY INTENSITY

We can also classify paradoxical interventions by their intensity. Omer distinguishes among strong, mild, and permissive interventions.[25] Permissive interventions, which are appropriate to nondirective psychodynamic therapies, reflect the therapist's understanding that the counselee may not be able to overcome the symptom, and it may reappear as necessary. A mild intervention highlights the positive nature of the symptom and is appropriate for moderately directive therapies. The directive therapist demands that the counselee increase the symptom level.

The degree to which an intervention intrudes into a person's life is on a continuum ranging from small and gradual to sudden, intense, and far-reaching.[26] The answer to the question of when is it appropriate to use small and gradual as opposed to intense and far reaching interventions correlates with the level of counselee flexibility: greater flexibility calls for more intense and far-reaching interventions while less flexibility demands milder interventions. People are least flexible in the symptomatic area and are more flexible as an intervention moves away from the symptomatic area. Less flexibility signals use of a milder intervention, and greater flexibility, a more intense, far-reaching intervention. A milder and smaller intervention would better suit the agoraphobic who has become housebound, but a stronger, more intrusive intervention fits the child who controls everyone around by throwing tantrums. The first situation calls for a mild change in the symptom itself, but the second indicates a radical change in the context of the problem. It's less threatening to change a person's situation than to ask him or her to change personal behavior. In other words, the further we move away from the symptom and the closer we get to the context or situation in which the problem occurs, the stronger the intervention.

Restraining the counselee's efforts to get rid of the problem is useful with several clinical problems, but it is especially effective in cases of general anxiety, performance anxiety, or where the counselee tries too hard to solve the problem.[27] While restraining is a paradoxical technique usually used to nurture the changes that occur as the result of other paradoxical interventions used, it can also serve as a primary intervention itself. An example of its use as a primary intervention is the family who came to therapy because their five-year-old boy had bowel movements in his pants.[28] At the close of the first interview the counselor wondered if there would be any negative consequences if the boy were toilet trained. The parents were sent home to think about this. When they returned for the second session, they were still unable to find any objectionable consequences that would result from the child's full recovery. The counselor had made a list of consequences and posed a few of them. Could the mother tolerate success? Would she become more successful than her mother, and would that be a problem? The mother thought not on both questions. How would she spend her extra time during the day? Each question exposed more about the relationships among the three people in the family. The counselor's questions made the parents wonder about their ability to be normal. Following this session, the father "firmly told him [the son] that if he did not have his bowel movement in the toilet he would be given castor oil and seated on the toilet until he did."[29] The following day the child performed properly. The third interview was canceled because the boy was using the toilet and the mother did not want to upset things. At the last contact with the family the situation remained improved and the counselor continued to "wonder" at how this change had come about.

Unlike the restraining intervention, the "go slow" approach does not ask for specific behavior such as trying to think of the consequences of being normal. This approach generally asks the counselee not to make any change he or she believes to be necessary because change may have disturbing repercussions. This intervention is useful for those who try too hard and with counselees who demand answers but are passive and resistant themselves.[30]

Paradoxical interventions are indicated for people who have a strong therapeutic relationship with the counselor and a normal sense of right and wrong. These people are basically free of paranoia and are not homicidal, suicidal, or in a crisis. The family systems should have a basic pattern of stability when paradox is applied.

TARGETS OF PARADOXICAL INTERVENTIONS

One writer suggests that paradoxical intervention is useful when there is a difference between what people are willing to do and what is actually done. While different people may express the willingness—the client, the family of the identified patient, or the counselor—"the paradoxical prescription will be most effective when directed at the agent of the unproductive attempt at behavior change."[31] By this Omer means that the person who is doing the willing becomes the target of the paradoxical intervention. This is illustrated in figure 11–1.

Willing   <———>   Doing   <———>   Context

Targets of Paradoxical Interventions
Figure 11–1

When the counselee wills the behavior to stop or decrease, a negative correlation is set up between what the counselee wills and what the counselee is doing. In a paradoxical intervention the counselor asks the counselee to reverse the direction of the willing—to want the opposite. For example, the parents of a tantrum-throwing child, who are willing the child to stop, should reverse their efforts. Milton Erickson illustrates such a reversal in his treatment of a thumb-sucking girl. Erickson asked the parents, who were doing the ineffectual willing, to solemnly promise that they would say nothing about thumb-sucking to their daughter for the next month. The girl was then encouraged to thumb-suck in the presence of her father and mother—to really take it out on them—but she was not aware of their promise not to respond. Although enthusiastic in the beginning, the girl stopped thumb-sucking when her efforts failed to get any results from her parents who had discontinued willing her to stop thumb-sucking.

Symptom prescription may also focus on the cognitive context. An example of this occurs when increased understanding is encouraged but change is restrained. When willing is *not* generating the doing, it is best to make changes in the symptom context rather than a symptom prescription. Of course, any contextual changes should be consistent with the counselor's theories and philosophies.[32]

Compliance-based strategies, those expecting the person to obey, interfere with any efforts the individual makes to stop or to restrain the unwanted behavior. Asking an obsessive person to obsess interferes with his or her efforts to stop obsessing. This makes the symptom lessen. On the other hand, defiance-based strategies instigate resistance which is, according to one theory, directly related to reactance—the desire to maintain individual freedom. The client stops the symptomatic behavior out of opposition to the counselor.

The client's desire to maintain his or her free will, combined with the voluntary quality of the behavior, as shown in figure 11–2, illustrates when compliance-based therapy is appropriate and when defiance-based therapy is appropriate. Defiance-based interventions take some aspect of the problem situation and exaggerate it into an ordeal. For example, the thumb-sucking girl cited above was asked to suck her thumb in front of her father for an hour and then in front of her mother for an hour. Making the assignment for an hour turned a spontaneous behavior into an ordeal that interfered with the symptom behavior.[33]

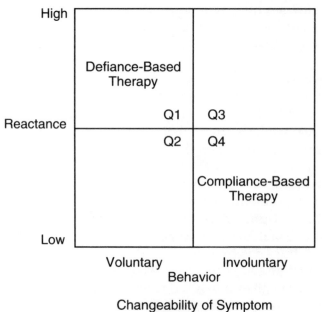

Changeability of Symptom
Figure 11–2

In Q4 of figure 11–2 the counselor uses compliance-based paradoxical interventions and asks for the individual to exaggerate, schedule, or in some other manner emphasize or intensify the symptomatic behavior. People in this category are cooperative and open to change. Some general justification for compliance-based changes include: (1) helping the counselee gain more control of the symptom—he or she must learn how to turn on the behavior before learning to turn it off; (2) predicting the onset of the symptom and scheduling it allows for its occurrence at the most convenient times; (3) gaining more understanding of why the symptom occurs, is especially appropriate for more sophisticated people.

At the other end of the spectrum, people who fit the pattern of defiance illustrated in Q1 are expected to disobey or modify any suggestion the counselor makes. Since the counselee is unlikely to describe the problem as voluntary or free to change, the intervention is best aimed at some supporting behavior that is open to change. The exception to this rule occurs when someone other than the counselee complains about the symptomatic behavior, as illustrated in the thumb-sucking case where the parents wanted the behavior to stop. The thumb-sucking was voluntary and, therefore, an appropriate target for change. It was successful because the parents were concomitantly influenced not to react as they had been in the past.

While the child exhibited the behavior, it was the parents who did the "willing." When they changed their behavior, the unwanted behavior stopped. In a way they became the target of the paradoxical intervention as illustrated earlier in figure 11–1.

Defiance-based interventions frequently target the voluntary behavior supporting the symptom. "If the likelihood of defiance is high, the therapist might actively *restrain* such patients from taking specific steps which, if taken, could lead to improvement."[34] With some defiant people the counselor might prescribe rather than restrain behavior. This intervention can disturb the support given by others in response to the complaints of the counselee, as in asking the hypochondriac to spend more time than usual rehearsing fears and concerns to the spouse.

The very defiant person may best respond to hard restraining. Hard restraining essentially and effectively limits the options or the belief that the problem is resolvable. Hard restraint was the core of the solution for a young man with an eleven-year-old sleep disorder. Out of a fear of missing reveille while in the military service, he developed a problem of very rarely sleeping through the night. After I listened to his story, he told me he did not want any of my crazy ideas. I responded, "We'll talk about this in four weeks; you are not ready to get over this problem yet." This remark implied he should continue having the symptom, which would mean he should lessen his efforts to mend his sleep problem. He recovered spontaneously that very day.

If counselors desire compliance in order to interrupt the symptom pattern, they must build interventions as an extension of and compatible with how counselees wish to view themselves. On the contrary, increasing defiance by building the directive in a way *incongruent* with the way counselees want to see themselves increases the likelihood that they cease the targeted symptom. Such was the case with a woman who suffered a severe loss. For a year she had been feeling depressed and sad. When she came for counseling, she was told that what she was experiencing was grief and, because grief has its own way of working itself out, no attempt should be made to keep it from happening. The counselor expressed concern about truncating the grief experience and advised her to go home and grieve as much as she felt necessary, instructions that were contrary to what others had told her and to what she was trying to do. Between sessions she grieved some but started to improve to the extent that even others noticed her improvement and encouraged her to recover further.

Between the two extremes are Q3 and Q2. People who fall into Q3, high reactance with involuntary behavior, are unlikely to respond to compliance-based interventions. However, it is possible to move them from defiance toward compliance if the counselor can reduce their reactance by being tentative, suggestive, and experimental in the intervention presentation. In most cases, they are more easily moved from Q3 to Q1. Such a move involves selecting for change some voluntary behavior that supports the symptom and thereby challenging their defiance. Another approach involves telling people you have a sure-fire solution but that you are unwilling to tell them until they promise they will carry it out no matter how difficult, inconvenient, or unreasonable it may seem.[35]

Encouraging the changes that result from compliance-based interventions follows the pattern of going slow, taking the time to solidify changes, and making sure that all ends are covered. Prescribing a relapse often encourages people to continue getting better. In one case a depressed counselee was encouraged to go home and even try harder to be depressed because therapy works when there is some symptom to work on. When he was not having the symptom he was not cooperating with the process of therapy, although such a result was what he sought from counseling. If people comply with the request for a relapse, it is done under the counselor's watchful eye, while the counselor displays skepticism or concern that the change may not last. With changes in defiance-based people the counselor must avoid praise by expressing skepticism and predicting that the change is only temporary.

People who are low in reactance and come to counseling with a voluntary problem (Q2) are best treated with straightforward problem-solving interventions until or unless they demonstrate reactance as the therapy progresses. One procedure discovers the pattern of the symptomatic behavior and interrupts that pattern with a change triggering counselees to decide whether they want to carry out the behavior or not. For example, the man who was concerned about his need to return to his house to check and recheck the lights, water, stove, etc., was instructed to check all he wanted, but when he returned to do so he was to remove his shoes *and* socks before proceeding. He stopped checking.

Another defiance-based tactic circumscribes the counselee's complaint-riddled communication. For the depressed person this would include saying, "With the situation you are describing I'm surprised you are not more depressed," instead of the usual, "Cheer up, things will certainly get better." Of course, this must be used carefully because such an intervention is contraindicated when the person is likely to comply and get more depressed simply because an "expert" has predicted it.

Paradoxical interventions may be positive or negative depending on their focus. While positive interventions call for symptom production, negative interventions impede improvement in the problem situation. A positive intervention asks people to produce the symptom under specified conditions. A negative intervention asks the counselee not to improve yet. Each is appropriate for different situations: when there is a physiological drive or concomitant, the negative or "go slow" intervention is more appropriate. For example, when a person has problems getting to sleep, the negative intervention retards efforts to sleep for a specified time period during which the physiological demand for sleep grows. When there is no physiological concomitant, as when a person suffers from phobias, unwanted thoughts, or jealousy, the positive intervention asks the client to produce the symptom under specified conditions. For example, you might say to the jealous person: "For the next week I want you to be as jealous as you can between 9 and 10 A.M." Such an intervention would call for symptom production at a time when the counselee did not usually have it.[36]

Breaking the symptom into its components—time, frequency, cognitive, behavioral, contextual, relational, attitudinal—permits prescribing the symptom in ways that differ from the manner the counselee usually experiences. Intensifying any component changes the symptom from involuntary to voluntary, meaning it is now amenable to change.[37]

> Try to do something that induces a change in the patient— any little change. Because the patient wants a change however small, and he will accept that as a change. He won't stop to measure the extent of that change. He'll accept that as a change and then follow that change and the change will develop in accordance with his own needs. It's much like rolling a snowball down a mountain side. It starts out a small snowball, but as it rolls down it gets larger and larger . . . and starts an avalanche that fits to the shape of the mountain.[38]

FINALLY

A change in feeling, thought, or behavior is what people seek when they come for counsel. To bring about change counselors must engage people by developing effective rapport, defining the problem as solvable, sifting out all previous attempts, establishing a goal, and then making an intervention if the problem has not been solved in an earlier stage of counseling. Helping people change is, indeed, something like starting a snowball rolling down a hill because we have no idea just where the change will take the counselee. It is true, however, that what they have been doing to solve the problem has not effected the kind and quality of life they want and, after all, making changes that bring success is what counseling is about.

NOTES

1. Michael Rohrbaugh, et al., "Compliance, defiance, and therapeutic paradox: Guidelines for strategic use of paradoxical interventions," *American Journal of Orthopsychiatry* 51, no. 3 (July 1981), 454–467.

2. Richard Driscoll, "Commonsense objectives in paradoxical interventions," *Psychotherapy* 22, no. 4 (Winter 1985), 774.

3. L. Seltzer, *Paradoxical Strategies in Psychotherapy: A comprehensive overview and guidebook* (New York: Wiley, 1986).

4. Gerald Weeks and Luciano L'Abate, *Paradoxical Psychotherapy: Theory and practice with individuals, couples, and families* (New York: Bruner/Mazel, 1982), 27.

5. Linda Riebel, "Paradoxical intention strategies: A review of rationales," *Psychotherapy* 21, no. 2 (Summer 1984), 266.

6. Haim Omer, "Integrating paradoxical interventions in the normal course of therapy: A nonspecific approach," *American Journal of Psychotherapy* 40, no. 4 (1986), 572–81.

7. Omer, "Integrating paradoxical interventions," 574.

8. Joseph Fabry, "Some practical hints about paradoxical intention," *International Forum for Logotherapy* 5, no. 1 (Spring/Summer 1982).

9. Fabry, "Practical hints," *International Forum for Logotherapy* 5, no. 1 (Spring/Summer 1982), 29.

10. D. Sean O'Connell, "Sympton prescription in psychotherapy," *Psychotherapy: Theory, Research and Practice* 20, no. 1 (Spring 1983), 16–17.

11. Glen Kercher and Darrell Smith, "Reframing paradoxical psychotherapy," *Psychotherapy* 22, no. 4 (1985), 786–92.

12. L. Festinger, *A Theory of Cognitive Dissonance* (Evanston, Ill.: Row, Peterson, 1957).

13. O'Connell, "Sympton prescription," 14.

14. Kercher and Smith, "Reframing paradoxical psychotherapy," 788–89.

15. G. Geothals, J. Cooper, and A. Naficy, "Role of foreseen, foreseeable and unforeseeable behavior in the arousal of cognitive dissonance," *Journal of Personality and Social Psychology* 39, (1979), 1179–85.

16. Kercher and Smith, "Reframing paradoxical psychotherapy," 789.

17. O'Connell, "Sympton prescription," 15–16.

18. Paul Watzwalick, J. Beavin, and Don Jackson, *Pragmatics of Human Communication* (New York: Norton, 1967), 213–15.

19. O'Connell, "Sympton Prescription," 15.

20. S. L. Garfield, *The Practice of Brief Psychotherapy* (New York: Pergamon, 1989), 25–27.

21. Watzwalick, Beavin, and Jackson, *Pragmatics of Human Communication*, 236.

22. O'Connell, "Sympton prescription," 18–19.

23. Omer, "Integrating paradoxical interventions," 579.

24. Driscoll, "Commonsense objectives," 775–78.

25. Omer, "Integrating paradoxical interventions," 577–78.

26. Omer, "Integrating paradoxical interventions," 578.

27. Anthoney Riordan, et al., "Understanding the use of paradox in counseling," *Family Therapy* 13, no. 3 (1986), 239–48.

28. Jay Haley, *Problem Solving Therapy: New strategies for effective family therapy* (San Francisco: Jossey-Bass, 1978), 142–47.

29. Haley, *Problem Solving Therapy*, 146.

30. Riordan, et al., "Understanding the use of paradox," 246.

31. Omer, "Integrating paradoxical interventions," 576.

32. Ibid. p. 574–75.

33. Jay Haley, *Ordeal Therapy* (San Francisco: Jossey-Bass, 1984).

34. Rohrbaugh, et al., "Compliance, defiance, and therapeutic paradox," 458, 462.

35. See Paul Watzlawick, John Weakland, and Richard Fisch, *Change: Principles of problem formation and problem resolution* (New York: Norton, 1974), 154–57; and Rohrbaugh, et al., "Compliance, defiance, and therapeutic paradox," 465.

36. Omer, "Integrating paradoxical interventions," 577.

37. Joel Katz, "Sympton prescription: A review of the clinical outcome literature," *Clinical Psychology Review* 4 (1984), 704.

38. D. Gordon and M. Meyers-Anderson, *Phoenix: Therapeutic patterns of Milton H. Erickson* (Cupertino, Calif.: Meta Publications, 1981), 122–23.

Epilogue

BEFORE YOU CLOSE THIS BOOK, let me review with you just where
we have come in trying to understand short-term counseling.
The five-stage model presented here is adapted from models
presented by Jay Haley and Allen Ivey.[1] Each stage offers the
counselor and counselee the opportunity to end counseling or
to build toward the subsequent stage, ending finally with an
intervention. You have probably puzzled and wondered your
way through the intricacies of helping people with such avant-
garde principles and techniques. Take time to ponder and
work some of what you have learned into your present way of
helping people. Do not expect to make an easy transition, but
dedicate yourself to effective and efficient means of helping
people.

But what about those people who need to be referred? Can
pastors determine early and quickly whether another professional is required? Obviously, requests which call for the

expertise of another profession should be referred immediately. There are, however, three questions counselors can ask of themselves as they conduct the first interview.[2] "What is the duration of the counselee's complaint?" is the first. Problems with long histories or recurring problems could alert the counselor to consider referring. The second, "What is the worst scenario?" raises the question of how extensively the complaint has affected the person's life. When there is little dysfunction or the counselee has fairly easily solved the problem in the past, there is a good chance you can help them now. If the dysfunction is severe, consider referral. The last question, "What is the best scenario?" looks for two items of information: how easily the problem has been solved in the past or what is the best the counselee has felt. When you discover negative or dismal responses on any of the criteria, and especially on all the criteria, think carefully about referring. Be prepared with a list of professional counselors in whom you have confidence.

If the answers to the three questions above are favorable, proceed to help the inquirer by using your God-prepared skills and some of the short-term counseling principles outlined in this book. Continue to prepare yourself because what is presented here is merely a sample of a vast literature on short-term counseling. Certainly counseling is part of the call to minister, and I pray you counsel effectively—and short-term.

NOTES

1. See Jay Haley, *Problem Solving Therapy: New strategies for effective family therapy* (San Francisco: Jossey-Bass, 1976), 15ff; and A. E. Ivey and W. J. Mathews, "A metamodel for structuring the clinical interview," *Journal of Counseling and Development* 63 (1984), 237–43.

2. James Gustafson, *The Complex Secret of Brief Psychotherapy* (New York: Norton, 1986), 281.

Bibliography

Anderson, C. M., and Susan Stewart. *Mastering Resistance: A practical guide to family therapy.* New York: Guilford, 1983.

Ascher, L. Michael, ed. "Relabeling or restructuring as a supportive therapeutic intervention in problems of academic stress." *Journal of College Student Personnel* (May 1983): 327–28.

Backus, W. *Telling the Truth to Troubled People.* Minneapolis: Bethany House, 1985.

Bandler, Richard, and John Grinder. *The Structure of Magic,* 2 vols. Palo Alto, Calif.: Science and Behavior Books, 1975.

Bandura, Albert. "Self-efficacy mechanisms in human agency." *American Psychologist* 3, no. 2 (1982): 140.

———. "Self-efficacy determinants of anticipated fears and calamities." *Journal of Personality and Social Psychology* 45, no. 2 (1983): 467.

———. "Self-efficacy: Toward a unifying theory of behavioral change." *Psychological Review* 84, no. 2 (1977): 193.

Bandura, Albert, Nancy Adams, and Janice Beyer. "Cognitive processes mediating behavioral changes." *Journal of Personality and Social Psychology* 35, no. 3 (March 1977): 126.

Bartunek, J. M., and M. K. Moch. "First-order, second-order, third-order change and organization development interventions: A cognitive approach." *Journal of Applied Behavioral Sciences* 23 (1988): 483–500.

Benshoff, James, and Harriet Glosoff. "Getting Clear: A model for problem definition in counseling." *American Mental Health Counselors Association Journal* 7, no. 4 (October 1985): 189.

Biehler, R. *Child Development: An introduction.* Boston: Houghton Mifflin, 1976.

Bigge, M. L. *Learning Theories for Teachers.* New York: Harper & Row, 1976.

Bolton, R. *People Skills: How to assert yourself to listen to others, and resolve conflicts.* Englewood Cliffs, N. J.: Prentice-Hall, 1979.

Brehm, J. W. *Response to Loss of Freedom: A theory of psychological reisitance.* Morristown, N. J.: General Learning Press, 1972.

Browning, Philip, and William Wright. "A Technique for problem identification in rehabilitation." *Rehabilitation Counseling Bulletin* 17, no. 1 (September 1973): 30.

Carlson, David. *Counseling and Self-Esteem.* Dallas, Tex.: Word, 1988.

Carson, Donald. *God With Us: Themes from Matthew.* Ventura, Calif.: Regal Books, 1985.

Cormier, William, and L. Sherilyn Cormier. *Interviewing Strategies for Helpers: Fundamental skills and cognitive behaviorial interventions.* Pacific Grove, Calif.: Brooks/Cole, 1991.

Corsini, Raymond, and Danny Wedding. *Current Psychotherapies.* Itasca, Ill.: F. E. Peacock, 1989.

Crabb, Larry, and D. Allender. *Encouragement: The key to caring.* Grand Rapids, Mich.: Zondervan, 1984.

Dayringer, R. *The Heart of Pastoral Counseling: Healing through relationship*. Grand Rapids, Mich.: Zondervan, 1989.

de Shazer, Steve. *Keys to Solution in Brief Therapy*. New York: Norton, 1985.

————. *Clues: Investigating solutions in brief therapy*. New York: Norton, 1988.

————. *Putting Difference to Work*. New York: Norton, 1991.

de Shazer, Steve, Insco Kim Berg, Eve Lipchik, Elam Nunnally, Alex Molnar, Wallace Gingerich, and Michele Weiner-Davis. "Brief therapy: Focused solution development." *Family Process* 25 (1986): 219.

Dinkmeyer, S., and L. E. Losoncy. *The Encouragement Book: Becoming a positive person*. New York: Prentice-Hall, 1987.

Dixon, D. N., and J. A. Glover. *Counseling: A problem-solving approach*. New York: Wiley, 1984.

Dolan, Yvonne. *A Path with a Heart: Ericksonian utilization with resistant and chronic clients*. New York: Bruner/Mazel, 1985.

Driscoll, Richard. "Commonsense objectives in paradoxical interventions." *Psychotherapy* 22 (Winter 1985): 774.

Dyer, Wayne. "A Goal-Setting Checklist for counselors." *Personnel and Guidance Journal* 55, no. 8 (1977): 470.

Dyer, Wayne, and John Vriend. *Counseling Techniques That Work*. American Association for Counseling and Development, 1988.

Edelstien, M. *Symptoms Analysis: A method of brief therapy*. New York: Norton, 1990.

Efran, Jay, M. Lukens, and R. Lukens. *Language, Structure, and Change: Frameworks of meaning in psychotherapy*. New York: Norton, 1990.

Egan, Gerard. *The Skilled Helper: A systematic approach to effective helping*. Pacific Grove, Calif.: Brooks/Cole, 1990.

Erickson, Milton H. "The 'surprise' and 'my-friend-John' techniques of hypnosis: Minimal cues and natural field experimentation." *American Journal of Clinical Hypnosis* 6, no. 299 (1964).

————. "Hypnotic approaches to therapy." *American Journal of Clinical Hypnosis* 20, no. 34 (1977b).

Erickson, Milton H., and E. Rossi. *Experiencing Hypnosis.* New York: Irvington, 1981.

Erickson, Milton H., and J. K. Zeig. *The Collected Papers of Milton H. Erickson on Hypnosis*, vol. 4. New York: Irvington, 1980.

Fabry, Joseph. "Some practical hints about paradoxical intention." *International Forum for Logotherapy*, vol. 5 (Spring/Summer 1982).

Festinger, L. *A Theory of Cognitive Dissonance.* Evanston, Ill.: Row, Peterson, 1957.

Fisch, R., J. H. Weakland, and L. Segal. *The Tactics of Change: Doing brief therapy.* San Francisco: Jossey-Bass, 1982.

Fischer, C. T. "Rapport as mutual respect." *Personnel and Guidance Journal* 48, no. 3 (1969).

Frank, J. "Therapeutic Components Shared by All Psychotherapies." In *Cognition and Psychotherapy*, edited by M. J. Mahoney and A. Freeman. New York: Plenum, 1985.

Fulghum, R. *All I Really Need to Know I Learned in Kindergarten.* New York: Ivy Books, 1989.

Garfield, S. *The Practice of Brief Psychotherapy.* Elmsford, N. Y.: Pergamon, 1989.

Geldenhuys, N. *Commentary on the Gospel of Luke.* Grand Rapids, Mich.: Eerdmans, 1951.

Genter, D. S. "A brief strategic model for mental health counseling." *Journal of Mental Health Counseling* 13, no. 1 (1991).

Gibson, Dennis. *Vitality Therapy.* Grand Rapids, Mich.: Baker Book House, 1989.

Goethals, G., J. Cooper, and A. Naficy. "Role of foreseen, foreseeable and unforeseeable behavioral consequences in the arousal of cognitive dissonance." *Journal of Personality and Social Psychology* 39 (1979): 1179–85.

Gordon, D., and M. Myers-Anderson. *Phoenix: Therapeutic patterns of Milton H. Erickson.* Cupertino, Calif.: Meta Publications, 1981.

Grosheide, F. W. *Commentary on the First Epistle to the Corinthians.* Grand Rapids, Mich.: Eerdmans, 1953.

Gustafson, James. *The Complex Secret of Brief Psychotherapy.* New York: Norton, 1986.

Hackney, Harold. "Goal-Setting: Maximizing the reinforcing effects of progress." *The School Counselor* (January 1973).

Haley, Jay. *Problem-Solving Therapy: New strategies for effective family therapy.* San Francisco: Jossey-Bass, 1976.

———. *Conversations with Milton H. Erickson, M.D.*, vol. 3, Changing Children and Families. New York: Norton, 1985.

———. *Ordeal Therapy.* San Francisco: Jossey-Bass, 1984.

Hayakawa, S. I. *Language in Thought and Action.* 4th ed. New York: Harcourt Brace Jovanovich, 1978.

Heard, Warren. "Second-Order Cybernetics and the Teachings of Jesus." Trinity Evangelical Divinity School, 1990.

Howard, G., D. Nance, and P. Myers. *Adaptive Counseling and Therapy: A systematic approach to selecting effective treatments.* San Francisco: Jossey-Bass, 1987.

Huber, Charles, and Barbara Backlund. *The Twenty Minute Counselor: Transforming brief conversations into effective helping experiences.* New York: Continuum, 1991.

Hughes, C. *Goal Setting: Key to individual and organizational effectiveness.* American Management Association, 1965.

Ivey, A. E., and N. Gluckstern. *Basic Influencing Skills: Participant manual.* Amherst, Mass.: Microtraining Associates, 1976.

Ivey, A. E., and W. J. Matthews. "A metamodel for structuring the clinical interview." *Journal of Counseling and Development* 63 (December 1984).

Jessee, Edgar, Gregory Jurkovic, Jeffrey Wilkie, and Michael Chiglinsky. "Positive reframing with children: Conceptual and clinical considerations." *American Journal of Orthopsychiatry* 52, no. 2 (April 1982): 317.

Kanfer, F., and B. Schefft. *Guiding the Process of Therapeutic Change.* Champaign, Ill.: Research Press, 1988.

Katz, Joel. "Sympton prescription: A review of the clinical outcome literature." *Clinical Psychology Review* 4 (1984): 704.

Keeny, B. P. *Aesthetics of Change.* New York: Guilford Press, 1983.

Kelly, G. A. *A Theory of Personality: The psychology of personal constructs.* New York: Norton, 1965.

Kercher, Glen, and Darrell Smith. "Reframing paradoxical psychotherapy." *Psychotherapy* 22 (1985): 786–92.

Kotesky, R. L. *General Psychology for Christian Counselors.* Nashville: Abington Press, 1983.

Kraft, Robert, Charles Claiborn, and E. Thomas Dowd. "Effects of positive reframing and paradoxical directives in counseling for negative emotions." *Journal of Counseling Psychology* 32, no. 4 (1985): 620.

LaClave, Linda, and Gregory Brack. "Reframing to deal with patient resistance: Practical application." *American Journal of Psychotherapy* 43 (January 1989): 68.

Lankton, Stephen, and C. Lankton. *The Answer Within: A clinical framework of Ericksonian hypnotherapy.* New York: Bruner/Mazel, 1983.

Lewis, C. S. *Out of a Silent Planet.* New York: Macmillan, 1965.

Lipchik, Eve. *Interviewing.* Rockville, Md.: Aspen, 1988.

Locke, E. A. and Latham, G. P. *Goal Setting: A motivational technique that works.* Englewood Cliffs, N. J.: Prentice-Hall, 1984.

Locke, Edwin, Karyll Shaw, Lise Saari, and Gary Latham. "Goal Setting and Task Performance: 1969–1980." *Psychological Bulletin* 90, no. 1 (1981): 125–52.

Losoncy, L. *Turning People On: How to be an encouraging person.* Englewood Cliffs, N. J.: Prentice-Hall, 1977.

Nezu, A., C. Nezu, and M. Perri. *Problem-Solving Therapy for Depression: Theory, research and clinical guidelines.* New York: John Wiley & Sons, 1989.

O'Connell, D. Sean. "Sympton prescription in psychotherapy." *Psychotherapy: Theory, Research and Practice* 20 (Spring 1983): 16–17.

O'Hanlon, Bill, and James Wilk. *Shifting Contexts: The generation of effective psychotherapy*. New York: Guilford, 1987.

O'Hanlon, William. *Taproots: Underlying principles of Milton Erickson's therapy and hypnosis*. New York: Norton, 1987.

O'Hanlon, William H., and M. Weiner-Davis. *In Search of Solutions: A new direction in psychotherapy*. New York: Norton, 1989.

Omer, Haim. "Integrating paradoxical interventions in the normal course of therapy: A nonspecific approach." *American Journal of Psychotherapy* 40, no. 4 (October 1989): 572.

Puig, Angelo. "Relabeling or restructuring as a supportive therapeutic intervention in problems of academic stress." *Journal of College Student Personnel* (May 1983): 273–74.

Riebel, Linda. "Paradoxical intention strategies: A review of rationales." *Psychotherapy* 21, no. 2 (Summer 1984): 266.

Riordan, Anthony, Norman Severinsen, Don Martin, and Maggie Martin. "Understanding the use of paradox in counseling." *Family Therapy* 13 (1986): 239–48.

Rogers, Carl. *On Becoming a Person*. Boston: Houghton Mifflin, 1961.

Rohrbaugh, Michael, Howard Tennen, Samuel Press, and Larry White. "Compliance, defiance, and therapeutic paradox: Guidelines for strategic use of paradoxical interventions." *American Journal of Orthopsychiatry* 51 (July 1981): 454–67.

Rosen, Sidney, ed. *My Voice Will Go with You: The teaching tales of Milton H. Erickson, M. D.* New York: Norton, 1982.

Rossi, E. L., ed. *The Collected Papers of Milton H. Erickson*, vol. 4. New York: Irvington, 1980.

Rossi, E. L., and O. M. Ryan, eds. *Life Reframing in Hypnosis: The Seminars, Workshops, and Lectures of Milton H. Erickson*, vol. 2. New York: Irvington, 1985.

Seltzer, L. *Paradoxical Strategies in Psychotherapy: A comprehensive overview and guidebook*. New York: John Wiley & Sons, 1986.

Shulman, Bernard H. *Contributions to Individual Psychology*. Chicago: Alfred Adler Institute, 1973.

Spencer, S., and J. Adams. *Life Changes: Growing through personal transitions*. San Luis Obispo, Calif.: Impact Publishers, 1990.

Talmon, Moshe. *Single-Session Therapy: Maximizing the effect of the first (and often only) therapeutic encounter*. San Francisco, Calif.: Jossey-Bass, 1990.

Thoresen, Carl, and Jane Anton. "Intensive Counseling." *Focus on Guidance* 6, no. 2 (October 1973): 4.

Watzlawick, Paul. *Munchhausen's Pigtail: or Psychotherapy and "reality" essays and lectures*. New York: Norton, 1990.

Watzlawick, Paul, ed. *The Invented Reality*. New York: Norton, 1984.

―――. *The Language of Change: Elements of therapeutic communications*. New York: Basic Books, 1978.

Watzlawick, Paul, J. Beavin, and Don Jackson. *Pragmatics of Human Communication: A study of interactional patterns, pathologies, and paradoxes*. New York: Norton, 1967.

Watzlawick, Paul, John Weakland, and Richard Fisch. *Change: Principles of problem formation and problem resolution*. New York: Norton, 1974.

Watzlawick, Paul, and John Weakland, eds. *The Interactional View: Studies at the Mental Research Institute, Palo Alto (1965–1974)*. New York: Norton, 1977.

Weeks, Gerald, and Luciano L'Abate. *Paradoxical Psychotherapy: Therapy and practice with individuals, couples, and families*. New York: Bruner/Mazel, 1982.

Weiner, M. F. *Practical Psychotherapy*. New York: Bruner/Mazel, 1986.

Wilk, James. "Ericksonian therapeutic patterns: A pattern which connects." In *Ericksonian Psychotherapy*, vol. 4, *Clinical*

Applications, edited by J. K. Zeig. New York: Bruner/Mazel, 1985.

Wolberg, Lewis R. *Handbook of Short-Term Psychotherapy*. New York: Thieme-Stratton, 1980.

Yapko, Michael. *When Living Hurts: Directives for treating depression*. New York: Bruner/Mazel, 1988.

Index